Crochet Christmas

Crochet Christmas

25 festive decorations to make

Jacki Donhou
Josephine Laurin
Angel Koychev

Contents

Introduction   6
Materials and tools   10
Stitches and techniques   12
Finishing touches   28
Abbreviations   29

34
Christmas Bell

38
Christmas Tree

42
Festive Star

46
Stocking

50
Wrapped Present

54
Wreath

58
Light Garland

62
Mistletoe

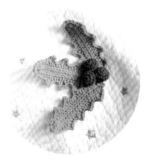

66
Holly

72
Penguin

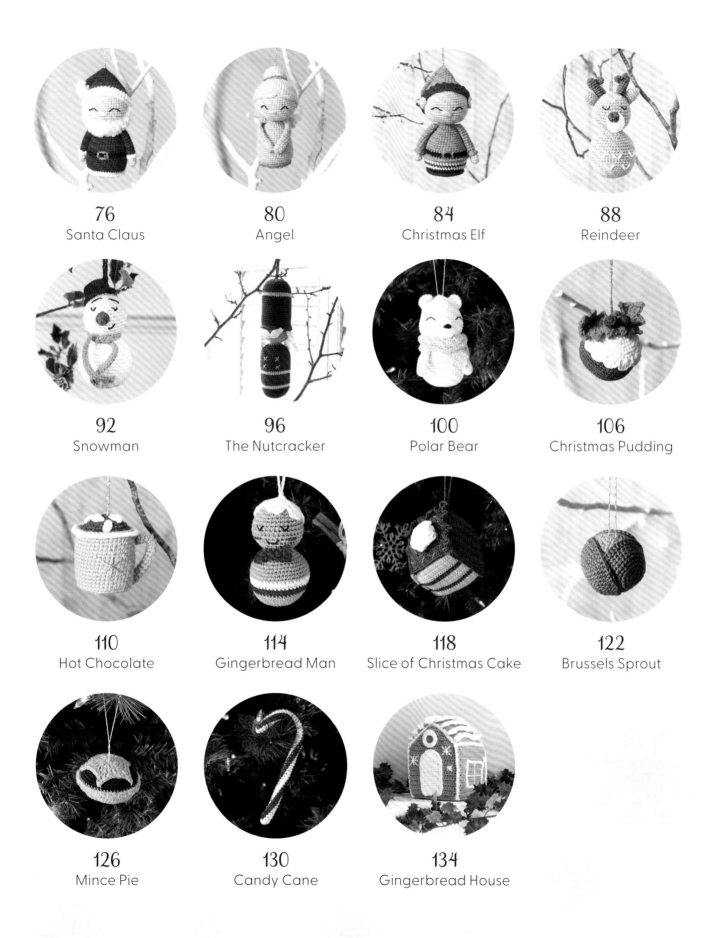

76
Santa Claus

80
Angel

84
Christmas Elf

88
Reindeer

92
Snowman

96
The Nutcracker

100
Polar Bear

106
Christmas Pudding

110
Hot Chocolate

114
Gingerbread Man

118
Slice of Christmas Cake

122
Brussels Sprout

126
Mince Pie

130
Candy Cane

134
Gingerbread House

Welcome

Christmas is the most wonderful time of the year, and nothing adds festive cheer to the holiday season like hand-crafted gifts and decorations.

This collection of 25 festive decorations to crochet is the perfect way to prepare for and celebrate Christmas. You'll find all the trimmings, from a Christmas Wreath and Holly to Mistletoe and a Light Garland; festive friends including a Penguin, a Polar Bear and Santa Claus himself; and those tasty treats we love at Christmas, from a healthy Brussels Sprout to a Gingerbread Man and the all-important Christmas Pudding.

Designed with beginner crocheters in mind, but perfect for even the most advanced maker, these projects use simple techniques including the amigurumi method of crocheting tightly in the round to craft beautiful creations quickly, perfect for last-minute gifts or sprucing up your festive décor.

Get ready for some oh-so-merry Christmas Crochet!

Materials, tools and techniques

Materials and tools

These are the materials and tools you will need to complete the colourful projects in this book.

YARN

Most of the projects in this book are made from cotton. Cotton is a soft, fluffy fibre that grows in a boll, or protective case, around the seeds of the cotton plant. In yarn form it comes in two broad types: mercerised and unmercerised. Mercerisation is a treatment that makes cotton more lustrous, with brighter colours. It tends to feel sleek and shiny, while unmercerised cotton will have a more matt appearance and a softer feel.

To add a little festive sparkle, there are some shiny, metallic and extra-fluffy yarns included in these projects. Most of these are made from manmade fibres such as polyester.

Most of these small projects will use only small amounts of yarn and you may well be able to make several projects from one 50g ball. Some of the yarns come in smaller balls, but where a project uses only a small amount of a yarn that comes in a larger, 100g ball, this has been listed as a small amount rather than as the whole ball.

If you use a different brand from the ones suggested in the projects, the makes may turn out differently from the photographs. Lighter-weight yarns will create smaller pieces, while thicker yarns will produce bigger projects.

CROCHET HOOKS

Crochet hooks come in a large range of sizes. Finding the right hook size for your project and choice of yarn can be difficult. The larger the hook, the larger your stitches will be. When working with amigurumi patterns, choosing a hook size two or three sizes smaller than what is recommended on the yarn label is ideal; this results in tighter stitches with smaller holes for the stuffing to show through.

In this book we have tended to go a little smaller than recommended, but not as small as for classic amigurumi. For instance, the recommended hook size for Hobbii Rainbow Deluxe 8/4 is 2.5-3.5mm, but as we wanted a tighter stitch, we chose to go down to a 2mm hook size.

Hook sizes are given in both European and US terms. In the case of a 3mm hook where there is no direct equivalent, two options are offered: C/2, or 2.5mm, and D/3, or 3.25mm. You may want to go for the smaller option to get a tighter tension for these projects.

CROCHET THREAD

Crochet thread is a very fine mercerised cotton yarn. It is not a thread used for sewing projects but is intended for delicate crochet and knitting crafts like lace work. It is mostly available in three thicknesses: size 3, size 10 and size 20, and in a range of colours. We used size 10 for our projects. It is thinner than a lightweight, fingering or 4 ply yarn and has the most colour options. It is good for embroidering details and adding hanging loops for tree decorations.

STUFFING

Polyester fibre filling is a synthetic hypoallergenic fibre made for pillows, crafts and toys. When you stuff a crocheted piece, you want it to be firm enough to hold its shape but not over-stuffed. Follow the steps clearly, as some pieces include instructions on how to stuff.

DARNING NEEDLES

Darning needles are long needles with a large eye used to sew together and attach the crocheted pieces. With our patterns, we tend to use two needles: a larger needle with a blunt tip to sew the pieces together, approximately 7in (17.5cm) in total length with an eye 1in (2.5cm) long; and a smaller needle with a sharp tip approximately 1½in (4cm) in total length for the embroidered details. If you find another size needle that works better for you, use the more comfortable size.

SCISSORS

Using a small pair of embroidery scissors with sharp tips is best. When you need to trim yarn ends after finishing off, smaller scissors lessen the risk of cutting through and damaging the other stitches.

SEWING PINS

Use these stick pins to keep all your crocheted parts secured and in place for sewing. Pins with a ball or a heart on the top are easier to use and give you something to hold. They are also easier to see against the crocheted surface. Pins with a flat top are not recommended, because they can get lost in your crocheted pieces. I like to use a lot of pins, so my pieces stay in the correct place and do not move while I am attaching them.

STITCH MARKERS

Stitch markers are plastic or metal clasps that hook on to your crochet work and keep track of either the starting or the ending stitch in your rounds. As you crochet, you can move your stitch marker up to the next round.

Stitches and techniques

Here we explain the crochet stitches and techniques you will need to be familiar with in order to make the projects in this book. With easy-to-follow instructions and clear illustrations, you'll be making the cutest Christmas crochet in no time.

HOLDING A HOOK

To hold a crochet hook, use your dominant hand to grip the hook and your less dominant hand to hold the yarn.

Hold the crochet hook at a downward angle, like a knife.

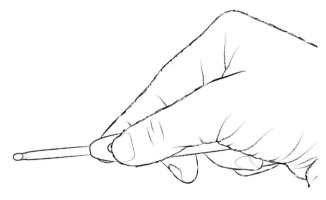

HOLDING YARN

There are many ways to hold the yarn while you crochet. It all depends on which hold is the most comfortable for you to maintain the right amount of tension.

If the yarn tension is too tight as you crochet, inserting the crochet hook into the next set of stitches could be difficult. If the tension is too loose, you will create holes in the rounds through which the stuffing could show. Take the time to find a hold that suits you.

Step 1: A simple way to hold the yarn is to begin by wrapping it around your little finger, then carry it under the next two fingers and over the index finger.

Step 2: Your thumb and middle finger will then grip the tail end of the yarn to hold it in place. Elevate your index finger to add the tension the yarn needs and make your first stitch.

MAKING A SLIPKNOT

Almost all pieces of crochet will begin with a slipknot.

Holding the yarn end, make a loop by crossing the yarn over itself. Insert the hook through the centre of the loop, yarn over the hook and pull the hook back through the centre. Pull the yarn end to tighten the loop on the hook to create the slipknot.

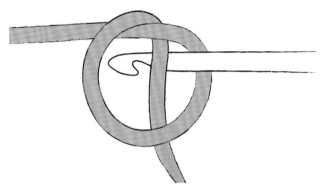

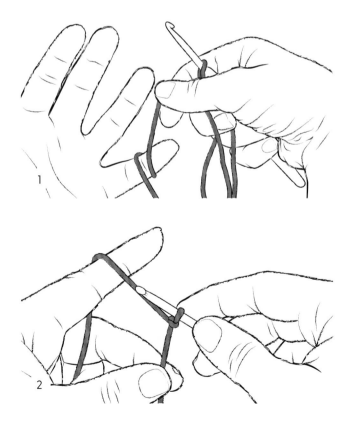

CHAIN STITCH (ch)

A chain stitch is a basic stitch that is mostly used to start or end a row.

Step 1: Starting with a slipknot, wrap the yarn around the crochet hook.

Step 2: Simply pull the yarn through the loop on the hook to form the first chain.

Step 3: If you need to make several chains, repeat the steps until you have the required number of chains.

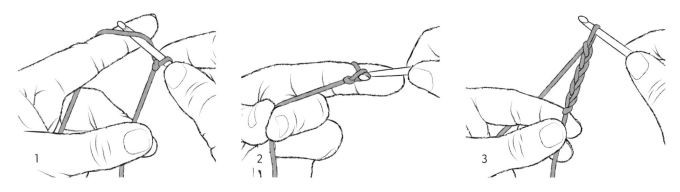

SLIP STITCH (sl st)

The slip stitch has more than one use in a pattern, adding a detailed seam to a piece and sometimes connecting pieces together.

Step 1: Insert the crochet hook under the stitch and wrap the yarn around the crochet hook.

Step 2: Pull the yarn through the stitch and through the loop on the crochet hook. If needing to make several slip stitches, repeat the steps until you have the correct number of slip stitches for the pattern.

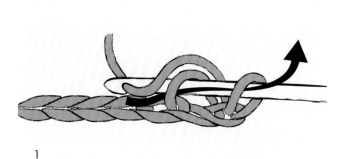

DOUBLE CROCHET (dc)

Double crochet is the main stitch used for the projects.

Step 1: Insert the crochet hook under both loops of the stitch or the chain space.

Step 2: Wrap the yarn around the crochet hook and pull the yarn through the stitch. There will be two loops on the crochet hook.

Step 3: Wrap the yarn around the crochet hook once more and pull the yarn through both loops on the crochet hook.

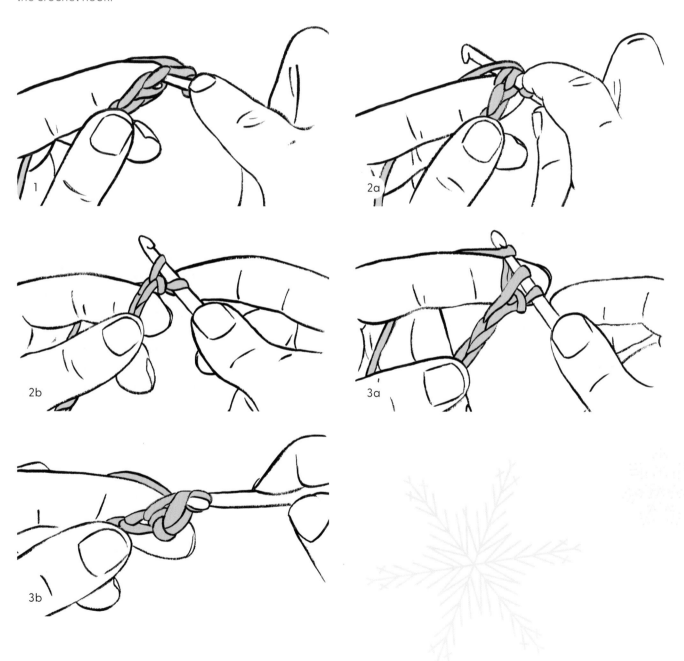

TREBLE (tr)

Treble stitch is a taller version of double crochet.

Step 1: Wrap the yarn around the crochet hook and then insert the hook under the stitch or the chain space.

Step 2: Wrap the yarn around the crochet hook and pull the yarn through the stitch. There will be three loops on the crochet hook. Wrap the yarn around the crochet hook again.

Step 3: Pull the yarn through two of the loops on the crochet hook, leaving two loops on the crochet hook. Then wrap the yarn around the hook once more.

Step 4: Pull the yarn through the two remaining loops on the crochet hook.

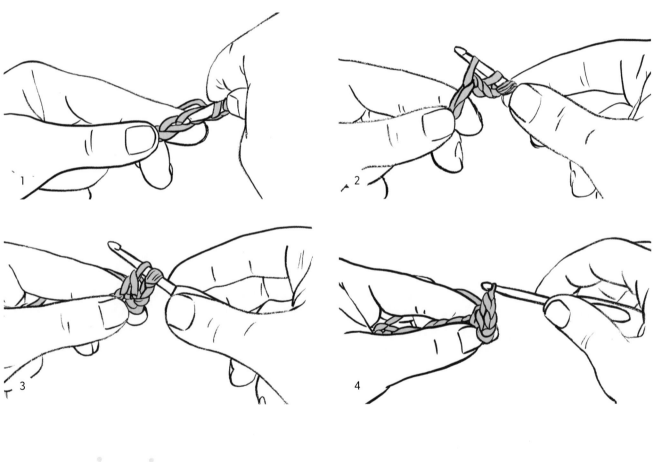

HALF TREBLE (htr)

Half treble stitch is similar to double crochet but starts by wrapping the yarn around the crochet hook at the beginning of the stitch.

Step 1: Wrap the yarn around the crochet hook, then insert the hook under the stitch or the chain space.

Step 2: Wrap the yarn around the crochet hook and pull the yarn through the stitch. There will be three loops on the crochet hook.

Step 3: Wrap the yarn around the crochet hook once more and pull the yarn through all three loops on the crochet hook.

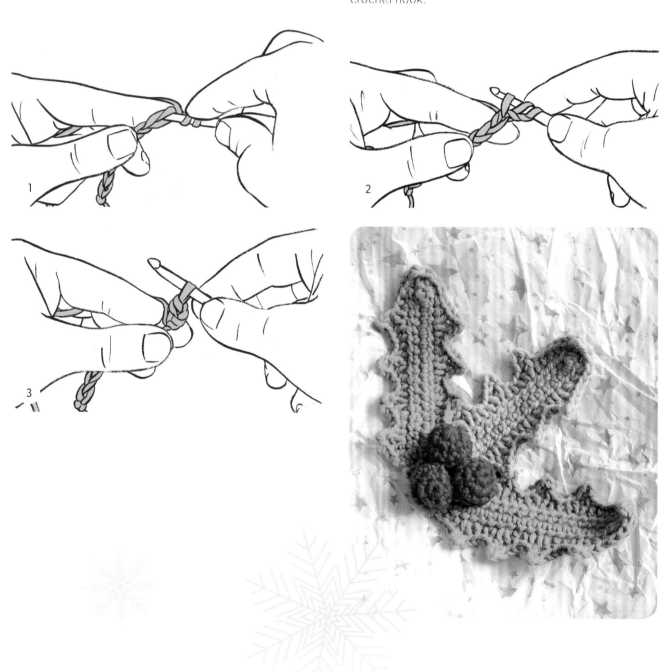

DOUBLE TREBLE (dtr)

Double treble stitch is an even taller stitch that starts by wrapping the yarn around the crochet hook two times at the beginning of the stitch.

Step 1: Wrap the yarn around the crochet hook twice.

Step 2: Insert the hook under the stitch or the chain space, wrap the yarn around the crochet hook and pull the yarn through the stitch. There will be four loops on the crochet hook.

Step 3: Wrap the yarn around the crochet hook again and pull the yarn through two of the four loops on the crochet hook. This will leave three loops on the crochet hook. Wrap the yarn around the crochet hook and pull the yarn through two of the three loops on the crochet hook, leaving two loops on the crochet hook.

Step 4: Wrap the yarn around the crochet hook once more and pull the yarn through the last two loops on the crochet hook to complete the stitch.

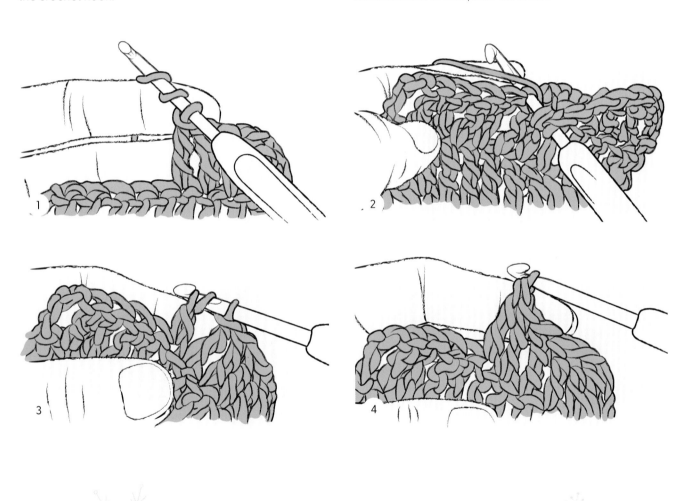

WORK TWO DOUBLE CROCHET STITCHES INTO THE NEXT STITCH TO INCREASE (dc2inc)

Working two dc stitches in the same space is a way to make a row or round larger (known as increasing).

Work two dc stitches into the same stitch or chain space. This will increase the stitch count by one dc stitch.

HALF TREBLE, TREBLE AND DOUBLE TREBLE INCREASES (htr2inc, tr2inc, dtr2inc)

Another way to increase a row or a round is to use two half treble stitches. Work two htr stitches into the same stitch or chain space. This will increase the stitch count by one htr stitch. To work a treble (tr2inc) or double treble (dtr2inc) increase, work in the same way but using treble or double treble stitches.

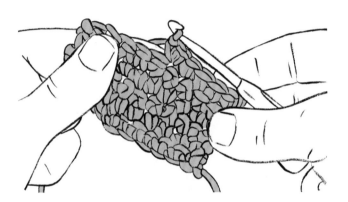

WORK TWO DOUBLE CROCHET STITCHES TOGETHER TO DECREASE (dc2tog)

A decrease is to crochet two stitches together to shorten a row or round. The method shown here is for an invisible decrease, where the front loops of the two stitches are pulled together so that the back loops collapse behind the stitch to close up the small hole and prevent the stuffing from showing.

Step 1: Insert the hook under the front loop only of the stitch. Then, insert the hook under the front loop only of the next stitch.

Step 2: With three loops on the hook, yarn over and pull through both the front loops. This leaves two loops on the hook. Yarn over and pull through the last two loops.

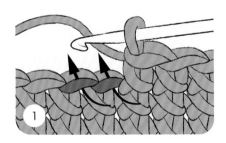

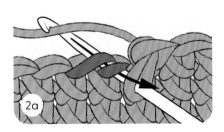

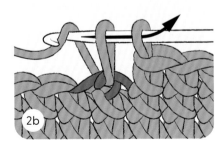

WORK TWO HALF TREBLE STITCHES TOGETHER TO DECREASE (htr2tog)

Another way to decrease in a row or round is to crochet two half treble stitches together, decreasing the stitch count by one.

Step 1: Wrap the yarn around the hook and insert the hook under the first st. Wrap the yarn around the hook again and draw the yarn up through the stitch. This leaves three loops on the hook.

Step 2: With three loops on the hook, repeat step 1: wrap the yarn around the hook and insert the hook under the second st. Then wrap the yarn again and draw it up through that st. This leaves five loops on the hook.

Step 3: Wrap the yarn around the hook for the last time and pull through all five loops.

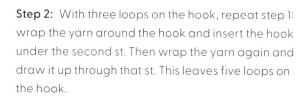

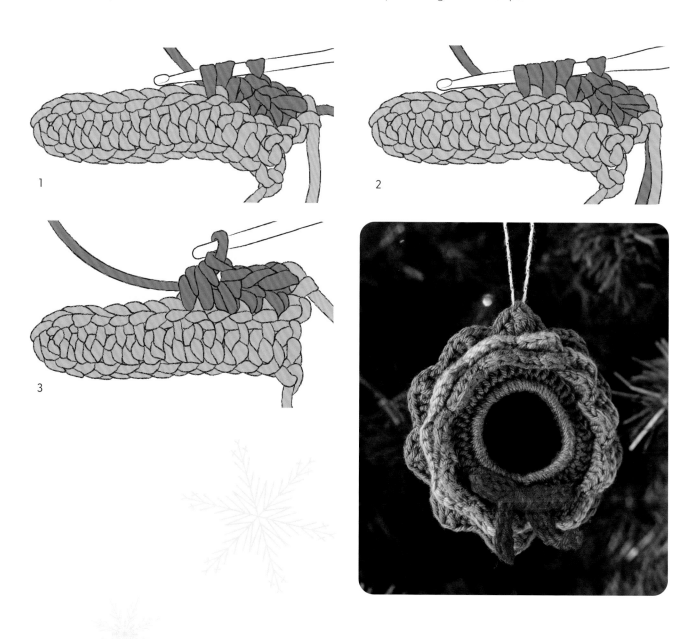

MAGIC CIRCLE (MC)

The magic circle or ring is the cleanest way to begin a round when crocheting, especially when making amigurumi. It is an adjustable ring with an end, usually made with double crochet stitches, that tightens to close the centre of the first round.

Step 1: Holding the yarn end, make a loop by crossing the yarn over itself. Then grip that crossing point, insert the hook through the centre of the loop, wrap the yarn around the crochet hook and pull the hook back through the centre.

Step 2: While still holding the circle, wrap the yarn around the crochet hook and pull the yarn through the loop on the hook to form the first chain. Then work around the circle as follows:

Step 3: Insert the crochet hook through the circle, wrap the yarn around the hook and pull the yarn through. There will be two loops on the crochet hook.

Step 4: Wrap the yarn around the crochet hook once more and pull the yarn through both loops on the crochet hook.

Step 5: This completes the first double crochet stitch on the magic circle. Repeat steps 3 and 4 until you have the right number of double crochet stitches for the pattern.

Step 6: Gently pull the yarn end to tighten and close the magic circle. In some designs, you will need to leave the magic circle open so you can stuff the piece.

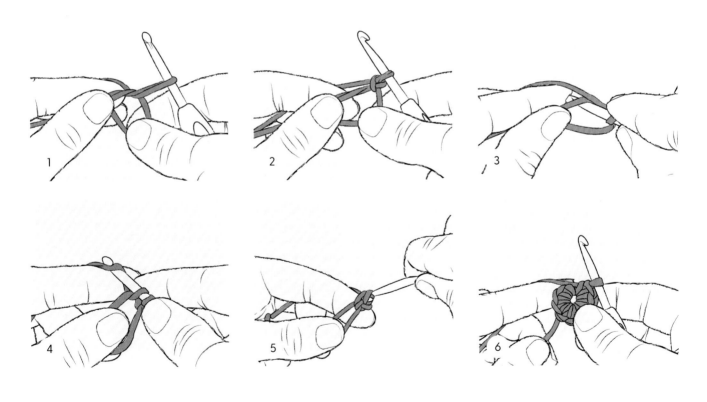

BACK LOOP ONLY (BLO)

The top of a stitch has two loops, a front loop and a back loop. The back loop is the loop that is the furthest from you and the only loop the crochet hook will work under, leaving the closest loop, the front loop, unworked. When working in the back loop only, it changes the effect of the piece you are working on. It reshapes your work and forces the stitches back from their original position. This happens at transitions in crocheted pieces. It also leaves the front loop visible so you can come back to it later and add a detail or edging, such as the branches of the Christmas Tree (page 38).

Insert the hook under the loop of the next stitch that is furthest away, not under both loops of the next stitch.

FRONT LOOP ONLY (FLO)

The front loop of the stitch is the loop that is closest to you and the only loop the crochet hook will work under, leaving the back loop unworked. When working FLO stitches, it changes the positioning of the stitches and curves your next rounds or rows forward.

Insert the hook under the loop of the next stitch that is nearest you, not under both loops of the next stitch.

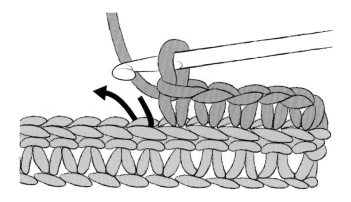 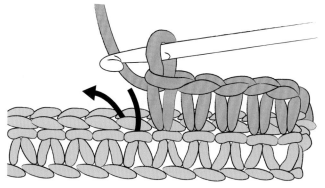

PUFF STITCH

Puff stitches are small, raised stitches crocheted to pop up and give a small textured detail. A puff stitch is made from a grouping of five unfinished, half double crochet stitches in the same stitch, which is then closed at the top to make them pop out.

Step 1: Yarn over and insert the hook under the next stitch. Yarn over and pull through the stitch. This leaves three loops on the hook.

Step 2: Yarn over and insert the hook under the same stitch. Yarn over again and pull through the stitch. Repeat these steps two more times until there are nine loops on the hook.

Step 3: Yarn over one last time and carefully pull through all nine loops. Then work one chain stitch to close the puff stitch.

CHANGING COLOURS

Colours are often changed from round to round or row to row, but in some cases, such as the Penguin and the Candy Cane, they are changed within a round.

Step 1: When you need to change a colour in a round, leave the last stitch of the previous colour unfinished without pulling the final loop through the stitch.

Step 2: Wrap the new colour around the hook and pull through the leftover loops.

Step 3: Continue the new colour in the next stitch or stitches. Tie the loose tails in a knot and leave them inside the crocheted piece.

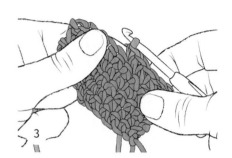

FASTEN OFF INVISIBLY IN A ROUND

Fastening off in a round can leave a noticeable bump. Choosing to do an invisible fasten-off will leave the stitches with a cleaner finish to the round.

Step 1: Cut the end of the yarn, leaving a yarn tail of about 4in (10cm). Pull the loop up and out of the last stitch.

Step 2: With a large embroidery needle, thread the tail through the eye of the needle. Before moving on, count the stitches in the round backwards and mark the first stitch of that round. Insert the needle under both of the top loops of the second stitch that is next to the marked stitch. This will overlap the first stitch, ensuring that we keep the same number of stitches in the round.

Step 3: Pull the needle up and insert it underneath the back loop of the last stitch in the round. This is the same stitch the yarn started from. Weave in the tail on the back or inside of the piece.

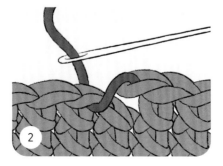
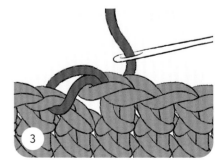

FASTEN OFF IN A ROW

Fastening off at the end of a row is very important. Leaving the tail end of the yarn exposed or loose can result in the piece unravelling and you losing all your hard work. Properly fastening off can prevent that from happening.

Cut the end of the yarn leaving a yarn tail of about 4in (10cm). Pull the tail up through the loop with the hook.

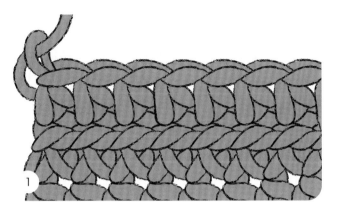

WEAVING IN THE ENDS AFTER SEWING

Weaving in loose ends is usually the final step in any crochet project, but sewing up all that leftover yarn can seem like a lot of work. In order not to get overwhelmed, it is best to weave in a few of the ends as you sew the pieces together.

Step 1: Thread a large embroidery needle with the end or yarn tail, then insert the needle through the crocheted piece and out at a location that is inconspicuous. Insert the needle underneath a few stitches along one of the rows or rounds.

Step 2: Pull the yarn slightly tight and then reverse to come back in the other direction under a few more stitches. Hide the remaining yarn tail in the piece.

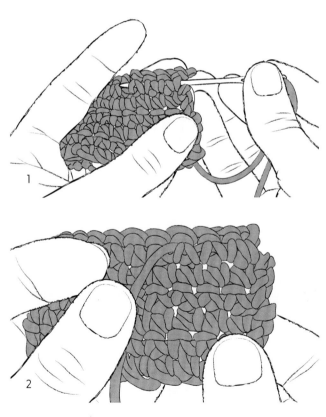

Finishing touches

This section teaches you how to sew all the pieces together and add details. It is the last step of completing your crochet so you can sit back and enjoy your accomplishments.

WHIP STITCH

Whip stitch is used to attach the pieces together. First make sure the two pieces are pinned against each other in the location the pattern states. Thread the large embroidery needle with the leftover tail of the first piece being attached, insert the needle under the stitch of the matched-up stitch on the second piece and pull it through. Next, bring the needle back up and under both loops of the next stitch on the piece that is being attached and pull it tight. Then insert the needle under the next stitch of the second piece. Repeat the steps until both pieces are secure.

MATTRESS STITCH

Step 1: First make sure the two pieces are pinned against each other in the location the pattern states. Thread a large embroidery needle with the leftover tail of the first piece, insert the needle under the stitch post or bar of the matched-up stitch on the second piece and pull it through tightly. The stitch post or bar is the yarn in between each round that connects the two.

Step 2: Insert the needle back through the same hole you started on the first piece and out under the next stitch post, then pull it though. Repeat the steps until both pieces are secure.

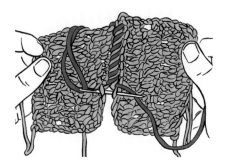
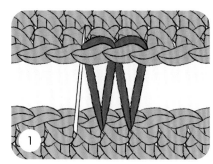
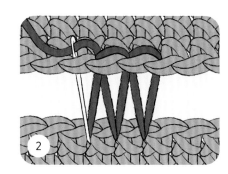

Abbreviations

The patterns in this book are written in UK crochet terms.

BLO	back loop only
ch	chain
cm	centimetre(s)
dc	double crochet
dc2inc	work 2 double crochet stitches into the next stitch to increase
dc2tog	work 2 double crochet sts together to decrease
dtr	double treble
FLO	front loop only
htr	half treble
htr2inc	work 2 htr sts into the next st to increase

htr2tog	work 2 htr sts together to decrease
in	inch(es)
m	metre(s)
MC	magic circle
rep	repeat
rnd	round
sl st	slip stitch
st(s)	stitch(es)
tr	treble
tr2inc	work 2 tr sts into the next st to increase
yd	yard(s)

The Designs

All the trimmings

Christmas Bell

The Christmas bell's melodious chime spreads joy and cheer, symbolising giving, togetherness and kindness during the holiday season, guiding souls towards love and peace.

SKILL LEVEL

FINISHED SIZE

2in (5cm)

SUPPLIES AND MATERIALS

Hobbii Rainbow Deluxe 8/4 100% Turkish cotton (approx 186yd/170m per 50g)
1 x 50g ball in 43 Pineapple (A)
1 x 50g ball in 59 Apple Red (B)
Ricorumi Lamé DK 62% polyester, 38% polyamide (approx 55yd/50m per 10g)
1 x 10g ball in 002 Gold (C)
2mm (US B/1) crochet hook
Stitch marker (optional)
Darning needle
Polyester filling
Scissors

PATTERN NOTE

The Bell is worked in continuous rounds and the Bow is worked in rows.

BELL

Rnd 1: With A, working into MC, 6 dc (6 sts).
Rnd 2: (Dc2inc) 6 times (12 sts).
Rnd 3: (1 dc, dc2inc) 6 times (18 sts).
Rnd 4: 1 dc, dc2inc, (2 dc, dc2tog) 5 times, 1 dc (24 sts).
Rnd 5: (3 dc, dc2inc) 6 times (30 sts).
Rnds 6-13: 1 dc in each st around (30 sts).
Rnd 14: (Dc2inc) 30 times (60 sts).
Cut yarn and fasten off yarn tail. With C, fold a 6in (15cm) yarn piece and make a knot on the ends, from the inside pull through the yarn in the middle.

BOW

Row 1: With B, 13 ch. Start in your second ch from hook, 1 dc in each ch, 1 ch, turn (12 sts).
Rows 2-5: BLO 1 dc in each st, 1 ch, turn (12 sts).
Row 6: BLO 1 dc in each st (12 sts).
Cut yarn leaving a long tail to wrap around middle of Bow.
Sew Bow to top of Bell.

Then, with the darning needle and either silver or gold crochet thread, add a large loop at the top of the Bell to hang from the Christmas tree. Whip stitch the thread under a st, at the back of the top of the Bow. Tie the two yarn ends together to complete the loop.

Christmas Tree

Let a wintry wonderland take over your home with a dazzling Christmas tree shining in the spotlight. Sprinkled with a touch of gold glam, it's the perfect canvas to unleash your imagination and create a glowing tapestry of holiday magic.

SKILL LEVEL

FINISHED SIZE

9in (23cm)

SUPPLIES AND MATERIALS

Premier Parfait Chunky 100% polyester (approx 131yd/120m per 100g)

1 x 100g ball in 1150-30 Emerald (A)

1 x 100g ball in 1150-12 Sunshine (B)

Ricorumi Lamé DK 62% polyester, 38% polyamide (approx 55yd/50m per 10g)

1 x 10g ball in 002 Gold (C)

3.5mm (US E/4) and 4mm (US G/6) crochet hooks

Stitch marker (optional)

Darning needle

Polyester filling

Scissors

Cardboard (optional)

PATTERN NOTES

The Branch placement photo opposite shows Tree made in a different yarn from the project, to show details better. All the Branches are made with the tip of the Tree facing you. After finishing each branch, cut the yarn and fasten off the yarn tail.

TREE

Rnd 1: With a 4mm crochet hook and A, working into MC, 8 dc (8 sts).
Rnd 2: (Dc2inc) 8 times (16 sts).
Rnd 3: (1 dc, dc2inc) 8 times (24 sts).
Rnd 4: (2 dc, dc2inc) 8 times (32 sts).
Rnd 5: (3 dc, dc2inc) 8 times (40 sts).
Rnd 6: (4 dc, dc2inc) 8 times (48 sts).
Rnd 7: BLO 1 dc in each st around (48 sts).
Cut out a round circle of cardboard that fits in the bottom of the circle.
Stuff as you go from here.
Rnds 8 and 9: 1 dc in each st around (48 sts).
Rnd 10: BLO 1 dc in each st around (48 sts).
Rnds 11-13: 1 dc in each st around (48 sts).
Rnd 14: BLO 1 dc in each st around (48 sts).
Rnd 15: 1 dc in each st around (48 sts).
Rnd 16: (4 dc, dc2tog) 8 times (40 sts).
Rnd 17: 1 dc in each st around (40 sts).
Rnd 18: BLO 1 dc in each st around (40 sts).
Rnds 19 and 20: 1 dc in each st around (40 sts).
Rnd 21: (8 dc, dc2tog) 4 times (36 sts).
Rnd 22: BLO 1 dc in each st around (36 sts).
Rnd 23: (7 dc, dc2tog) 4 times (32 sts).
Rnd 24: 1 dc in each st around (32 sts).
Rnd 25: (6 dc, dc2tog) 4 times (28 sts).
Rnd 26: BLO 1 dc in each st around (28 sts).
Rnd 27: (5 dc, dc2tog) 4 times (24 sts).
Rnd 28: 1 dc in each st around (24 sts).
Rnd 29: (4 dc, dc2tog) 4 times (20 sts).
Rnd 30: BLO 1 dc in each st around (20 sts).
Rnd 31: (3 dc, dc2tog) 4 times (16 sts).
Rnd 32: 1 dc in each st around (16 sts).

Rnd 33: (2 dc, dc2tog) 4 times (12 sts).

Rnd 34: BLO 1 dc in each st around (12 sts).

Rnd 35: (1 dc, dc2tog) 4 times (8 sts).

Rnd 36: 1 dc in each st around (8 sts).

Cut yarn and close the hole using the FLO.
Fasten off.

BRANCHES

Position the branches as shown in placement photo.

Branch 1

Rnd 1: With A, pull up a loop in the FLO, 1 ch, dc in the same st, skip 1 st, 5 tr in the next st, (skip 1 st, 1 dc, skip 1 st, 5 tr in the next st) 11 times, sl st into the first dc (72 sts).

Rnd 2: Change to C and a 3.5mm hook. Dc2inc in each st around (144 sts).

Branch 2

Rnd 1: With A, pull up a loop in the FLO, 1 ch, dc in the same st, skip 1 st, 5 tr in the next st, (skip 1 st, 1 dc, skip 1 st, 5 tr in the next st) 11 times, sl st into the first dc (72 sts).

Rnd 2: Change to C and a 3.5mm hook. Dc2inc in each st around (144 sts).

Branch 3

Rnd 1: With A, pull up a loop in the FLO, 1 ch, dc in the same st, skip 1 st, 5 tr in the next st, (skip 1 st, 1 dc, skip 1 st, 5 tr in the next st) 9 times, sl st into the first dc (60 sts).

Rnd 2: Change to C and a 3.5mm hook. Dc2inc in each st around (120 sts).

Branch 4

Rnd 1: With A, pull up a loop in the FLO, 1 ch, dc in the same st, skip 1 st, 5 tr in the next st, (skip 1 st, 1 dc, skip 1 st, 5 tr in the next st) 8 times, sl st into the first dc (54 sts).

Rnd 2: Change to C and a 3.5mm hook. Dc2inc in each st around (108 sts).

Branch 5

Rnd 1: With A, pull up a loop in the FLO, 1 ch, dc in the same st, skip 1 st, 5 tr in the next st, (skip 1 st, 1 dc, skip 1 st, 5 tr in the next st) 6 times, sl st into the first dc (42 sts).

Rnd 2: Change to C and a 3.5mm crochet hook. Dc2inc in each st around (84 sts).

Branch 6

Rnd 1: With A, pull up a loop in the FLO, 1 ch, dc in the same st, skip 1 st, 5 tr in the next st, (1 dc, skip 1 st, 5 tr in the next st) 4 times, sl st into the first dc (30 sts).

Rnd 2: Change to C and a 3.5mm hook. Dc2inc in each st around (60 sts).

Branch 7

Rnd 1: With A, pull up a loop in the FLO, 1 ch, dc in the same st, skip 1 st, 5 tr in the next st, (1 dc, skip 1 st, 5 tr in the next st) twice, sl st into the first dc (18 sts).

Rnd 2: Change to C and a 3.5mm hook. Dc2inc in each st around (36 sts).

STAR

Rnd 1: With B, (1 dc, 1 tr, 2 ch, 1 tr) 5 times (25 sts).

Pull together tightly. Cut yarn and leave a tail.
Sew the Star to the top of the Tree.

Festive Star

Light up your Christmas tree with a touch of celestial charm! This delightful amigurumi ornament is perfect for beginners and experienced crocheters alike. Choose vibrant colours or metallic yarn for a truly festive touch.

SKILL LEVEL

●

FINISHED SIZE

5½ x 5½in (14 x 14cm)

SUPPLIES AND MATERIALS

Hobbii Friends Cotton 8/4 Mercerised 100% mercerised cotton (approx 174yd/160m per 50g)

1 x 50g ball in 105 Emerald (A)

1 x 50g ball in 108 Pistachio (B)

2mm (US B/1) crochet hook

Darning needle

Scissors

PATTERN NOTE
Make 3 Star Sides using A and 3 Sides using B.

STAR SIDE (MAKE 3 IN A AND 3 IN B)
With A or B, 19 ch.
Row 1: Htr in second ch from hook and in all rem ch, turn (18 sts).
Row 2: 2 ch (doesn't count as a st), tr2inc in first st, htr2inc in next st, htr in all rem sts until 2 are left, htr2inc in next to last st, tr2inc in last st, turn (22 sts).
Row 3: Rep row 2 (26 sts).
Row 4: Rep row 2 (30 sts).
Row 5: 3 ch (doesn't count as a st), (1 dtr, 1 tr) in first st, htr2inc in next st, htr in all rem sts until 2 are left, htr2inc in next to last st, (1 tr, 1 dtr) in last st (34 sts).
Fasten off, cut and weave in your tail.

ASSEMBLY
Once you have made all six Star Sides, weave in all the loose ends and join them in groups of three, alternating the colours.

Join all short lateral sides as shown in pairs, with a row of dc, each having their WS facing each other, starting from inside, going towards the Side's points and placing 2 dc in that point. This will help you have a pointier end. Once this is done, you will have created two triangle-shaped frames.

Stop before you join your last two pieces on the second triangle.

Intertwine the still open triangle around the closed one, alternating passing over and under.

Refer to the picture to get the idea for the final shape.

Once the two triangles are intertwined, sew together the last two pieces.

To make a loop for hanging the ornament, join the colour you prefer to one of the top six corners of the Star with a sl st, (1 ch, 1 dc) in same st and make as many ch as you like. I suggest you do that until you have a string of about 6in (15cm). Sl st in the last dc you made, fasten off, cut and weave in your tail.

Stocking

Bring a touch of whimsical charm to your holiday décor with this adorable Christmas stocking! Whether you hang it on your tree, garland several together or offer them as personalised gifts, these ornaments are sure to spread holiday cheer. Choose from a variety of festive colours, grab your hook, gather your yarn and crochet your way to a heartwarming Christmas filled with miniature magic.

SKILL LEVEL

FINISHED SIZE

4¾ x 8½ x 2½in (12 x 22 x 6cm)

SUPPLIES AND MATERIALS

Hobbii Friends Cotton 8/4 Mercerised 100% mercerised cotton (approx 174yd/160m per 50g)

1 x 50g ball in 40 Tomato or 104 Shamrock (A)

1 x 50g ball in 001 White (B)

2mm (US B/1) crochet hook

Darning needle

Polyester filling

Scissors

PATTERN NOTES

Make two identical Stocking pieces following the instructions. For the first piece yarn A is red, for the second piece yarn A is green, and yarn B is always white. When changing from A to B, do not cut the unused yarn, leave it on the side and bring it up while making the rows to be used again. The strands will be worked over while adding the Border later on.

While you are working on your two pieces there won't be an actual RS or WS as the stitches look the same on both sides.

STOCKING (MAKE 2)

Row 1: With A, 21 ch, dc in second ch from the hook and in all rem sts, turn (20 sts).

Row 2: 1 ch, htr in first and in all rem sts, turn (20 sts).

Rows 3 and 4: Rep row 2 (20 sts).

Change to B on next 1 ch, do not cut A.

Rows 5-8: With B, rep row 2 (20 sts).

After row 6, bring up A and twist it around B before making initial 1 ch of row 7, so it will get closer to the next colour change.

Change to A on next 1 ch, do not cut B.

Rows 9-12: With A, rep row 2 (20 sts).

After row 10, bring up B and twist it around A before making initial 1 ch of row 11, so it will get closer to the next colour change.

Change to B on next 1 ch, do not cut A.

Rows 13-16: With B, rep row 2 (20 sts).

After row 14, bring up A and twist it around B before making initial 1 ch of row 15, so it will get closer to the next colour change.

Change to A on next 1 ch, do not cut B.

Rows 17-20: With A, rep row 2 (20 sts).

After row 18, bring up B and twist it around A before making initial 1 ch of row 19, so it will get closer to the next colour change.

Change to B on next 1 ch, do not cut A (always rep this part from now on).

Row 21: With B, 1 ch, htr in first and in all rem sts until next to last one, 2 htr in last st, turn (21 sts).

Row 22: 1 ch, 2 htr in first st, htr in all rem sts, turn (22 sts). Bring up A and twist it around B before making initial 1 ch of row 23, so it will get closer to the next colour change (always rep this part from now on).

Row 23: Rep row 21 (23 sts).

Row 24: Rep row 22 (24 sts).

Row 25: With A, rep row 21 (25 sts).

Row 26: Rep row 22 (26 sts).

Row 27: Rep row 21 (27 sts).

Row 28: Rep row 22 (28 sts).

Row 29: With B, rep row 21 (29 sts).

Row 30: Rep row 22 (30 sts).

Row 31: Rep row 21 (31 sts).

Row 32: Rep row 22 (32 sts).

Rows 33–36: With A, rep row 2 (32 sts).

Row 37: With B, htr2tog, htr in all rem sts until 2 sts rem, htr2tog, turn (30 sts).

Row 38: Rep row 37 (28 sts).

Row 39: Rep row 37 (26 sts).

Row 40: Rep row 37 (24 sts). Fasten off B, cut B and weave in the end.

Row 41: With A, rep row 37 (22 sts).

Row 42: Rep row 37 (20 sts).

Row 43: Rep row 37 (18 sts).

Row 44: Rep row 37 (16 sts). Fasten off A, cut A and weave in the end.

BORDER (MAKE 2)

At this point, you need to decide which are the right and wrong sides of your Stocking. Lay the two pieces flat, pointing in opposite directions. The sides facing you will be the RS, so each piece will be the opposite of the other. With RS facing you, join B to the top left corner st with a sl st, 1 ch. Dc in same st. Dc in all lateral sts (there is no exact number of sts to make, but try to place them evenly all around the Stocking. The only recommendation is to make the same number on the first and the second piece. For me, it was a total of 160 sts and two 2 ch spaces, yours can vary). Dc in all bottom side sts and all lateral sts on the other side until you reach the top right corner, where you can place (1 dc, 1 ch, 1 dc). Dc in all

rem sts on the top side, placing (1 dc, 1 ch) in the last st (the first st you worked in), sl st to first dc made, skipping initial 1 ch. On the side where you brought your yarn up every four rows, work dc over the visible yarn so it will be hidden. Fasten off, cut yarn and weave in the end.

ASSEMBLY

Place the two pieces one on top of the other, wrong sides facing each other. For easier counting and matching, use stitch markers around the Borders to place the two pieces correctly together.

Join B in the top left corner, inserting your hook through both pieces' Border 1 ch spaces. (1 ch, 1 dc) in same space, dc in all rem sts of the Borders, always inserting the hook through both layers. When you reach the top right corner, you can place (1 dc, 1 ch, 1 dc) in the Borders' 1 ch space. At this point, stuff the Stocking and cont placing dc in all rem sts of the top side, placing (1 dc, 1 ch) in the top left corner 1 ch space, then joining with a sl st to your first st made. Fasten off, cut yarn and weave in the end.

In the top right corner, join B with a sl st. Dc in same st. Now make as many ch as you like. This will be used as a hanging loop. I suggest you do that until you have a string of about 6in (15cm). Sl st in the last dc you made, fasten off, cut yarn and weave in the end.

Wrapped Present

This charming pattern lets you create adorable wrapped present ornaments. Imagine your tree adorned with miniature gifts, each one a unique expression of your creativity. Hang these adorable wrapped presents on your tree, garland them together for a whimsical touch or wrap them up for heartfelt gifts.

SKILL LEVEL

●

FINISHED SIZE

3¼ x 3¼in (8.5 x 8.5cm)

SUPPLIES AND MATERIALS

Hobbii Friends Cotton 8/4 Mercerised 100% mercerised cotton (approx 174yd/160m per 50g)

1 x 50g ball in 63 Lilac (A)

1 x 50g ball in 47 Pink (B)

2mm (US B/1) crochet hook

Darning needle

Polyester filling

Scissors

PATTERN NOTE

While working on your Present pieces, there won't be a RS or WS, since the stitches look the same on both sides.

PRESENT SIDE (MAKE 6)

Row 1: With A, 21 ch, dc in second ch from the hook and in all rem sts, turn (20 sts).
Row 2: 1 ch, dc in first and in all rem sts, turn (20 sts).
Rows 3-21: Rep row 2 (20 sts).
Fasten off, cut yarn and weave in the end.
Your piece should be a square and meas around 2¾in (7.2cm) per side. If you need to, in order to get a square shape, you can add or subtract rows with the same pattern rep as above. Furthermore, if you wish to make a bigger or smaller Present, add more or fewer sts per row, and more or fewer rows per square.

ASSEMBLY

You can now join all six identical Present Sides together in order to create a cube. When you are almost done and have around 10 sts left to join on your last side, fill the Present with stuffing before finishing the last joining sts.

You can choose to use A for joining, so your cube will be in only one colour, or you can use B as a contrast. I have chosen B for this example.

Start by placing two pieces one on top of the other. Join the yarn with a sl st to any corner st (every corner st will always have a dc, a 1 ch space and another dc on the next side in the joining).

1 ch, dc in same st and all rem sts (or sides of rows, in every row of dc you should place 1 dc) on the side until the last one, going through both pieces.

1 ch, do not work on your second piece anymore, instead place your third piece.

Cont joining the first and third pieces: you will place 1 dc in the same st where you placed your previous dc on the

first piece, going through the corresponding first st of your third piece before that, then dc in all rem sts on that side until the last one, through both layers.

1 ch, then rep the same steps for your fourth and fifth pieces. This way, your first piece will be joined on all four sides to the other four pieces. Fasten off, cut yarn and weave in the end.

Cont joining the opposite sides of pieces 2, 3, 4 and 5 from the ones already joined, to each side of piece 6. Remember, always work through two layers, putting (1 dc, 1 ch, 1 dc) in each corner. Fasten off, cut yarn and weave in the end.

Now you are left with four sides of the cube that still need joining: as before, dc in all sts of each side. This time there is no need to place 1 ch in the corners, simply fasten off, cut yarn and weave in the ends each time.

Present string

To be sure of the length you need for your string, take a long piece of B and wrap it around the Present, finishing with a bow on top and leaving free tails. Then measure that piece of yarn. In my case, it was around 67in (170cm).

Make as many ch as needed (I made 371) until you reach that length, keeping in mind that, in this case, less isn't more – meaning that it's better to have the string longer than shorter!

Once you have made your ch, htr in second ch from hook and in all rem chs (I made 370), fasten off, cut yarn and weave in the ends. Wrap the string around the Present.

ORNAMENT OPTION

To make a loop for hanging the ornament, join whichever colour yarn you prefer to one of the top four corners of the cube with a sl st, dc in the same st, make as many ch as you like. I suggest you do that until you have a string of about 6in (15cm). Sl st in the last dc, fasten off, cut yarn and weave in the end.

Wreath

A Christmas wreath handmade from evergreen branches and decorated with small seasonal items like ribbons, pine cones and holly berries is traditionally hung on front doors during the festive season. This miniature version will be truly evergreen.

SKILL LEVEL

FINISHED SIZE

2¾in (7cm)

SUPPLIES AND MATERIALS

Hobbii Rainbow Deluxe 8/4 100% Turkish cotton (approx 186yd/170m per 50g)

1 x 50g ball in 38 Crocodile (A)

1 x 50g ball in 39 Fern (B)

1 x 50g ball in 59 Apple Red (C)

Silver or gold crochet thread

2mm (US B/1) crochet hook

Stitch markers

Darning needle

Polyester filling

Sewing pins

PATTERN NOTE

The Wreath is worked in continuous rounds and the Bow is worked in rows.

WREATH

Rnd 1: With A, 20 ch, sl st to the first ch to join (20 sts).
On the next rnd, the dc sts will be worked around the chain to make a solid ring.

Rnd 2: 42 dc around the ch, sl st to join, 2 ch (45 sts).

Rnd 3: Tr in each st around, sl st to join, 1 ch (44 sts).
On the next rnd, work FLO on each st in the rnd.

Rnd 4: FLO dc, (htr2inc, tr2inc, htr2inc, sl st) 10 times, sl st to join (73 sts).
Fasten off and weave the yarn tail into the Wreath.
Attach B to the leftover BLO of rnd 3 and cont to rnd 5.

Rnd 5: 1 dc in each st around, sl st, 1 ch, turn (44 sts).
After turning, work BLO on each st in the next rnd.

Rnd 6: BLO dc in the second st from the hook, (htr2inc, tr2inc, htr2inc, sl st) 10 times, sl st to join (72 sts).
Fasten off and weave the yarn tail into the Wreath.
Turn the Wreath to face forward and attach A to the leftover new BLO of rnd 5 and cont to rnd 7.

Rnd 7: BLO dc, (tr2inc, dtr2inc, tr2inc, dc) 10 times, sl st to join (72 sts).
Fasten off and weave the yarn tail into the Wreath.

BOW

Row 1: With C, 36 ch, turn (36 sts).

Row 2: 1 dc in each st along (35 sts).
Fasten off and leave a long tail for attaching.
Fold the long chain in thirds, crossing the right end over the left and pressing the crossed section up against the back part of the chain. Cut a long piece of yarn and wrap it around the centre of the crossed chain with the cut yarn piece about five times, tie a knot in the back with the two yarn ends to hold the Bow in place.

ASSEMBLY

Attach the Bow to the front of the lower part of the Wreath. Using the darning needle, add three or four whip stitches to the back of the Bow and the sts that start and end rnd 2 of the Wreath. Weave the extra yarn ends into the back of the Bow.

Then, with the darning needle and either silver or gold crochet thread, add a large loop at the top of the Wreath to hang from the Christmas tree. Whip stitch the thread under a st, on the top of the back ruffle. Tie the two yarn ends together to complete the loop.

Light Garland

Christmas lights are the hallmark of the holiday season, bringing warmth and lighting up the chilly nights of December. They transform the outsides of ordinary homes into charming attractions that make everyone want to stop and take in their beauty.

SKILL LEVEL

●

FINISHED SIZE
90 x 3in (228 x 7.5cm)

SUPPLIES AND MATERIALS
For full size
Hobbii Rainbow 8/6 100% cotton (approx 115yd/105m per 50g)
1 x 50g ball in 54 Yellow (A) 1 x 50g ball in 100 Deep Jungle Green (B)
1 x 50g ball in 31 Blue (C) 1 x 50g ball in 84 Green (D)
1 x 50g ball in 58 Red (E)
3mm (US C/2 or D/3) crochet hook
For ornament size
Hobbii Rainbow Deluxe 8/4 100% Turkish cotton (approx 186yd/170m per 50g)
1 x 50g ball in 43 Pineapple (A) 1 x 50g ball in 37 Forest (B) 1 x 50g ball in 23 Zenith Blue (C)
1 x 50g ball in 39 Fern (D) 1 x 50g ball in 59 Apple Red (E)
Silver or gold crochet thread (optional)
2mm (US B/1) crochet hook
Stitch marker (optional
Darning needle
Polyester filling
Scissors

PATTERN NOTE

The Christmas Lights are worked in rounds.
Stuff as you crochet.
For the Garland String all stitches are worked in a chain.
The tension on the chain stitches needs to be tight to ensure the bulbs are evenly spaced.

CHRISTMAS LIGHTS

Rnd 1: With A, working into MC, 6 dc (6 sts).
Rnd 2: 1 dc in each st around (6 sts).
Rnd 3: (Dc2inc) 6 times (12 sts).
Rnd 4: 1 dc in each st around (12 sts).
Rnd 5: (Dc, dc2inc) 6 times (18 sts).
Rnd 6: 1 dc in each st around (18 sts).
Rnd 7: (Dc, dc2inc, dc) 6 times (24 sts).
Rnds 8-10: 1 dc in each st around (24 sts).
Rnd 11: (3 dc, dc2inc) 6 times (30 sts).
Rnds 12-16: 1 dc in each st around (30 sts).
Rnd 17: (3 dc, dc2tog) 6 times (24 sts).
Rnds 18 and 19: 1 dc in each st around (24 sts).
Rnd 20: (Dc, dc2tog, dc) 6 times (18 sts).
Fasten off and weave in the extra yarn end into the piece. Attach B to the back of the light bulb on the last st of rnd 20.
Rnd 21: 1 dc in each st around (18 sts).
Rnds 22-24: BLO dc in each st around (18 sts).
Rnd 25: BLO (dc, dc2tog) 6 times (12 sts).
Fasten off, weave the yarn under each FLO and pull tight to close the hole.
Make one more Christmas Light in A, then six more Christmas Lights: two in C, two in D and two in E. This completes a full set of eight Christmas Lights to attach to the garland.

GARLAND STRING

Step 1: With A, start the Garland String with a long tail to add a loop for hanging, then 100 ch. Choose the first Christmas Light to secure to the Garland String.
Step 2: Sl st to the FLO of rnd 24 on the top of the Christmas Light, 4 ch, sl st to the FLO on rnd 24 directly across from the first sl st. Make sure there are 8 FLO sts on either side of the sl sts. This will ensure that the Christmas Light is attached evenly. 25 ch before attaching the next Christmas Light.
Repeat step 2 until there are seven Christmas Lights on the Garland.
Step 3: Sl st to the FLO of rnd 24 on the top of the last Christmas Light, 4 ch, sl st to the FLO on rnd 24 directly across from the first sl st. Make sure there are 8 FLO sts on either side of the sl sts. 100 ch to end the Garland String, leaving a long tail to add a loop for hanging.

ORNAMENT OPTION

If you chose to make the Christmas Lights in the smaller ornament size, omit the Garland String instructions. Instead, with the darning needle and either silver or gold crochet thread, add a large loop at the top of each Christmas Light to hang it from the Christmas tree. Enter the needle on the right side of rnd 25 and exit on the left side of the same rnd. Tie the two yarn ends together to complete the loop.

Mistletoe

Mistletoe is a symbol of love and romance. It's a staple of Christmas celebrations when it is hung above doorways and archways as a decoration in the home. This little plant has a special place in our hearts, as it's traditional to steal a kiss beneath it, for a little festive romance!

SKILL LEVEL

FINISHED SIZE
7½in (19cm)

SUPPLIES AND MATERIALS
For full size
Hobbii Rainbow 8/6 100% cotton (approx 115yd/105m per 50g)
1 x 50g ball in 23 Green (A) 1 x 50g ball in 001 White (B)
1 x 50g ball in 009 Nougat (C)
3mm (US C/2 or D/3) crochet hook
For ornament size
Hobbii Rainbow Deluxe 8/4 100% Turkish cotton (approx 186yd/170m per 50g)
1 x 50g ball in 39 Fern (A) 1 x 50g ball in 01 White (B) 1 x 50g ball in 06 Mocha Latte (C)
Silver or gold crochet thread
2mm (US B/1) crochet hook
Stitch markers
Darning needle
Polyester filling
Scissors
Sewing pins

PATTERN NOTES

The Mistletoe Branches are worked in rows. When turning, place the first dtr in the third ch from the hook. The Berries are worked in rounds. Slightly stuff each Berry before closing.

MISTLETOE BRANCHES (MAKE 5)
Leaf 1

With A, 31 ch, turn, working back up the ch to make the first leaf, dtr in the third ch from the hook, dtr, 3 tr, 3 htr, 4 dc.

This completes Leaf 1. Do not cut the yarn but cont with the chains in the next set of instructions to make the other Leaves.

Leaves 2 and 3

(21 ch, turn, dtr in the third ch from the hook, dtr, 3 tr, 3 htr, 4 dc) twice. Do not cut the yarn.

At this point there should be three Leaves on the long chain. Next you will work Leaf 4, then work the 6 dc sts up the chain to create a thick stem on the other side of the chain.

Leaf 4

15 ch, turn, working back up the ch to work Leaf 4, dtr in the third ch from the hook, dtr, 3 tr, 3 htr, 5 dc.

Do not cut the yarn but cont with the chains in the next set of instructions to make the other Leaves.

Leaves 5 and 6

(Dc 6 up the ch, then 15 ch, turn, dtr in the third ch from the hook, dtr, 3 tr, 3 htr, 5 dc, dc2inc in the next ch between the two Leaves) twice, 16 dc up the ch, sl st (226 sts).

Fasten off and tie the yarn ends together, then weave them into the Mistletoe Branches.

BERRIES (MAKE 6)

Rnd 1: With A, working into MC, 6 dc (6 sts).
Rnd 2: (Dc2inc) 6 times (12 sts).
Rnds 3 and 4: 1 dc in each st around (12 sts).
Rnd 5: (Dc, dc2tog) 4 times (8 sts).
Weave the yarn under each FLO, pull tight to close the hole.
Fasten off and leave a long tail for attaching.

ASSEMBLY

The Berries will be attached to three of the five Mistletoe Branches. Pin two of the Berries to the centre of the Mistletoe Branch where the two Leaves meet in the middle. The placement can be random between the top, middle or bottom Leaves. With the darning needle, whip stitch the Berries to the Mistletoe Branches until they are secure.

Gather the five Mistletoe Branches together in a cluster, then cut a long piece of yarn C and wrap it around the top of the Branches 8 times, about 7–8 sts down from the ends. Then tie the ends together and trim them.

ORNAMENT OPTION

With the darning needle and either silver or gold crochet thread, add a large loop at the back of the yarn C on the Branches to hang the ornament from the Christmas tree. Whip stitch the thread under the wrapped yarn C. Tie the two yarn ends together to complete the loop.

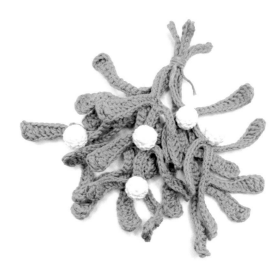

Holly

With its spiky, thick green leaves and deep red berries, holly would be hung around doorways and windows for good luck. Now it's used as a festive decoration to spruce up a fireplace mantel or add greenery to the holiday table.

SKILL LEVEL

FINISHED SIZE

4½ x 6in (11.5 x 15cm)

SUPPLIES AND MATERIALS

For full size

Hobbii Rainbow 8/6 100% cotton (approx 115yd/105m per 50g)

1 x 50g ball in 22 Dark Green (A)

1 x 50g ball in 84 Light Green (B)

1 x 50g ball in 58 Red (C)

3mm (US C/2 or D/3) crochet hook

For ornament size

Hobbii Rainbow Deluxe 8/4 100% Turkish cotton (approx 186yd/170m per 50g)

1 x 50g ball in 37 Forest (A)

1 x 50g ball in 39 Fern (B)

1 x 50g ball in 59 Apple Red (C)

Polyester filling

Stitch markers

Darning needle

Scissors

Sewing pins

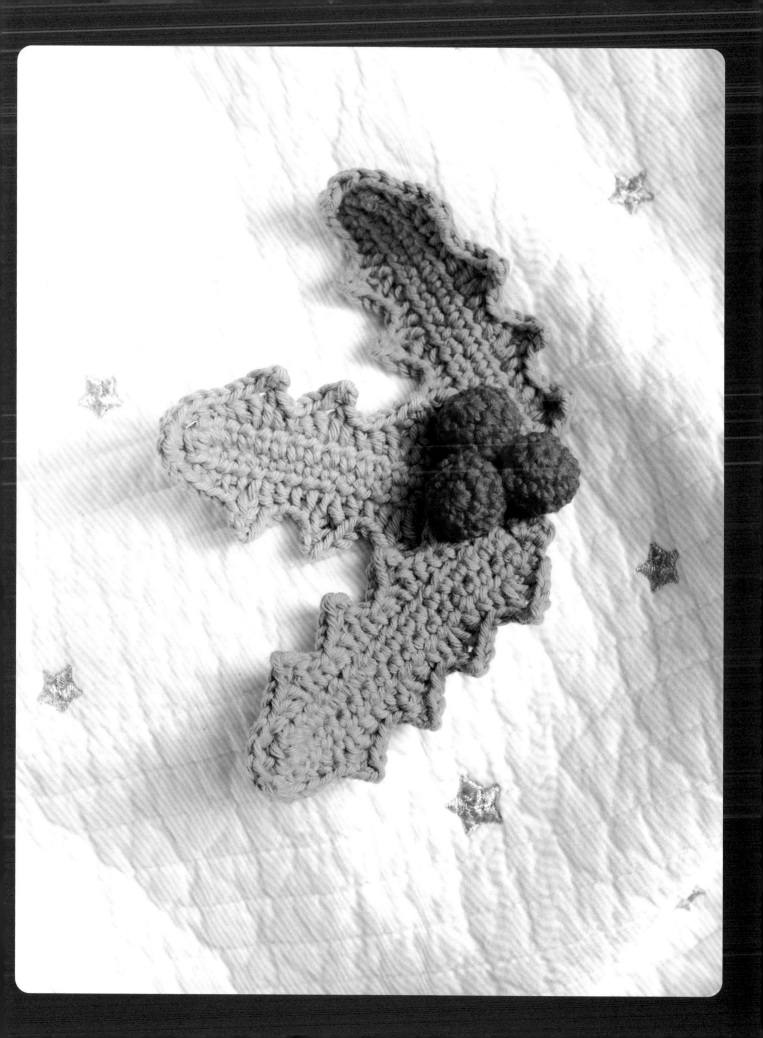

PATTERN NOTES

The Leaves are worked in rows. When turning, place the first dc in the second st from the hook. The Berries are worked in rounds. Slightly stuff each Berry before closing.

HOLLY LEAVES

Row 1: Using A, 21 ch, turn (21 sts).
Row 2: 2 dc, 17 htr, (3 htr) in the same st, 17 htr, 2 dc, 1 ch, turn (42 sts).
Row 3: 2 dc, 1 htr, (1 tr, 3 ch, 1 dc in the third ch from hook, 1 tr in the same st as the first tr, 1 htr, 1 dc, 1 htr) 4 times, 1 htr, 1 tr, 3 ch, 1 dc in the third ch from hook, 1 tr in the same st as the first tr, 2 htr, 1 dc, 1 htr, (1 tr, 3 ch, 1 dc in the third ch from hook, 1 tr in the same st as the first tr, 1 htr, 1 dc, 1 htr) 3 times, 1 tr, 3 ch, 1 dc in the third ch from hook, 1 tr in the same st as the first tr, 1 htr, 1 dc, sl st (86 sts).
Fasten off and leave a long tail for attaching.
Using the darning needle, weave in the extra yarn tail from the starting chain.
Make two more Holly Leaves, one in A and one in B, to complete a full set of three Holly Leaves.

BERRIES (MAKE 3)

Rnd 1: With C, working into MC, 6 dc (6 sts).
Rnd 2: (Dc2inc) 6 times (12 sts).
Rnd 3: (Dc, dc2inc) 6 times (18 sts).
Rnd 4: (Dc, dc2tog) 6 times (12 sts).
Rnd 5: (Dc, dc2tog) 4 times (8 sts).
Weave the yarn under each FLO, pull tight to close the hole.
Fasten off and leave a long tail for attaching.

ASSEMBLY

Layer the two dark green Holly Leaves on top of the bottom portion of the light green Holly Leaf, with the light green in the centre. Match up the lower 6 sts of rnd 3 of the right and left Leaves and angle them outwards from the centre Leaf.

Use pins to secure them in place, and with the darning needle and the leftover yarn end from the dark green Leaves, whip stitch the dark green Leaves on to the centre light green Leaf.

Flip the Leaves over and whip stitch the bottom section of the light green Leaf to the back side of the dark green Leaves. When the three Leaves are sewn together, weave in any extra yarn ends.

The three red Berries should be clustered and centred on the bottom of the three Holly Leaves. With the darning needle, attach the first Berry at the bottom of the two dark green Leaves and centre with three whip stitches.

Attach the other two Berries above the first, side by side. After securing the second Berry, add one or two whip stitches to the first Berry so there are no gaps between them. Add the last Berry and whip stitch it to the other Berries. Once finished, weave in the extra yarn ends.

ORNAMENT OPTION

If you choose to make the Holly Berries in the smaller ornament size, use the darning needle and either silver or gold crochet thread to add a large loop at the top of the central Holly Leaf. Whip stitch the thread under a stitch, on the top of the Leaf. Tie the two yarn ends together to complete the loop.

Festive friends

Penguin

This cheerful little penguin celebrates Christmas in style with its bright red scarf.

SKILL LEVEL

FINISHED SIZE
3in (8cm)

SUPPLIES AND MATERIALS
Hobbii Rainbow Deluxe 8/4 100% Turkish cotton (approx 186yd/170m per 50g)

1 x 50g ball in 11 Slate (A)

1 x 50g ball in 59 Apple Red (B)

1 x 50g ball in 02 Natural White (C)

Hobbii Rainbow 8/4 100% cotton (approx 174yd/160m per 50g)

1 x 50g ball in 57 Orange (D)

Ricorumi Lamé DK 62% polyester, 38% polyamide (approx 55yd/50m per 10g)

1 x 10g ball in 002 Gold (E)

Black embroidery thread

2mm (US B/1) crochet hook

Stitch marker (optional)

Darning needle

Polyester filling

Scissors

PATTERN NOTE
This pattern is worked in continuous rounds unless otherwise stated.

HEAD AND BODY
Rnd 1: With A, working into MC, 6 dc (6 sts).
Rnd 2: (Dc2inc) 6 times (12 sts).
Rnd 3: (1 dc, dc2inc) 6 times (18 sts).
Rnd 4: 1 dc, dc2inc, (2 dc, dc2inc) 5 times, 1 dc (24 sts).
Rnd 5: (3 dc, dc2inc) 6 times (30 sts).
Rnd 6: 2 dc, dc2inc, (4 dc, dc2inc) 5 times, 2 dc (36 sts).
Rnd 7: (5 dc, dc2inc) 6 times (42 sts).
Rnd 8: 3 dc, dc2inc, (6 dc, dc2inc) 5 times, 3 dc (48 sts).
Rnd 9: With A 19 dc, with C 3 dc, with A 4 dc, with C 3 dc, with A 19 dc (48 sts).
Rnd 10: With A 18 dc, with C 4 dc, with A 4 dc, with C 4 dc, with A 18 dc (48 sts).
Rnd 11: With A 17 dc, with C 6 dc, with A 2 dc, with C 6 dc, with A 17 dc (48 sts).
Rnds 12 and 13: With A 16 dc, with C 7 dc, with A 2 dc, with C 7 dc, with A 16 dc (48 sts).
Rnds 14-17: With A 16 dc, with C 16 dc, with A 16 dc (48 sts).
Rnd 18: With A 3 dc, dc2tog, 6 dc, dc2tog, 3 dc, with C 3 dc, dc2tog, 6 dc, dc2tog, 3 dc, with A 3 dc, dc2tog, 6 dc, dc2tog, 3 dc (42 sts).
Rnd 19: (5 dc, dc2tog) 6 times (36 sts).
Rnd 20: 2 dc, dc2tog, (4 dc, dc2tog) 5 times, 2 dc (30 sts).
Rnd 21: (3 dc, dc2tog) 6 times (24 sts).
Rnd 22: 1 dc, dc2tog, (2 dc, dc2tog) 5 times, 1 dc (18 sts).
Rnd 23: 1 dc in each st around (18 sts).
Rnd 24: 1 dc, dc2inc, (2 dc, dc2inc) 5 times, 1 dc (24 sts).
Rnd 25: (3 dc, dc2inc) 6 times (30 sts).
Rnds 26-28: 1 dc in each st around (30 sts).
Rnd 29: 2 dc, dc2inc, (4 dc, dc2inc) 5 times, 2 dc (36 sts).
Rnds 30-33: 1 dc in each st around (36 sts).

Rnd 34: 2 dc, dc2tog, (4 dc, dc2tog) 5 times, 2 dc (30 sts).
Rnd 35: (3 dc, dc2tog) 6 times (24 sts).
Rnd 36: (1 dc, dc2tog) 8 times (16 sts).
Rnd 37: (Dc2tog) 8 times (8 sts).
Cut yarn and fasten off the yarn tail.

WINGS (MAKE 2)
Rnd 1: With A, working into MC, 6 dc (6 sts).
Rnd 2: (1 dc, dc2inc) 3 times (9 sts).
Rnds 3-6: 1 dc in each st around (9 sts).
Rnd 7: 1 dc, leave the rem sts unworked. Flatten the Wing and dc through both sides to close the Wing.
Cut yarn and leave a long tail for sewing.
Place and sew the Wings to the side of the Body at rnd 26.

SCARF
Row 1: With B, 50 ch, start in the third ch from hook, 1 dc in each ch (48 sts).
Cut yarn and fasten off the yarn tail.
Tie the Scarf around the Penguin's neck.

FEET (MAKE 2)
Rnd 1: With D, 6 dc in MC (6 sts).
Rnd 2: 2 sl st, (sl st, 2 tr, sl st) 3 times, 1 sl st (15 sts).
Cut yarn and leave a long tail for sewing.
Place and sew the Feet under the Body with the toes pointing forwards.

ASSEMBLY
With E, add a loop at the top of the Penguin's head so it can hang on the tree.
With D, embroider a beak between rnds 13 and 14 on the Head.
With black embroidery thread, embroider 2 eyes over rnd 13 on the Head.

Santa Claus

Santa Claus symbolises Christmas with his joyful presence, red suit and generosity.
He embodies kindness, goodwill and the holiday spirit of love and giving.

SKILL LEVEL
● ● ●

FINISHED SIZE
5in (12.5cm)

SUPPLIES AND MATERIALS
Hobbii Rainbow Deluxe 8/4 100% Turkish cotton (approx 186yd/170m per 50g)

1 x 50g ball in 04 Winter White (A)

1 x 50g ball in 59 Apple Red (B)

1 x 50g ball in 02 Natural White (C)

1 x 50g ball in 09 Dark Chocolate (D)

Ricorumi Lamé DK 62% polyester, 38% polyamide (approx 55yd/50m per 10g)

1 x 10g ball in 002 Gold (E)

Cygnet Yeti 100% acrylic (approx 170yd/156m per 100g)

Small amount in 2001 Avalanche (F)

2mm (US B/1) and 4mm (US G/6) crochet hooks

Black embroidery thread

Stitch marker (optional)

Darning needle

Polyester filling

Scissors

This pattern is worked in continuous rounds, apart from the Beard which is worked in rows.

Use a 2mm crochet hook unless otherwise stated.

HEAD

Rnd 1: With A, working into MC, 6 dc (6 sts).
Rnd 2: (Dc2inc) 6 times (12 sts).
Rnd 3: (1 dc, dc2inc) 6 times (18 sts).
Rnd 4: 1 dc, dc2inc, (2 dc, dc2inc) 5 times, 1 dc (24 sts).
Rnd 5: (3 dc, dc2inc) 6 times (30 sts).
Rnd 6: 2 dc, dc2inc, (4 dc, dc2inc) 5 times, 2 dc (36 sts).
Rnd 7: (5 dc, dc2inc) 6 times (42 sts).
Rnd 8: 3 dc, dc2inc, (6 dc, dc2inc) 5 times, 3 dc (48 sts).
Rnds 9-13: 1 dc in each st around (48 sts).
Rnd 14: (7 dc, dc2inc) 6 times (54 sts).
Rnds 15-18: 1 dc in each st around (54 sts).
Rnd 19: (7 dc, dc2tog) 6 times (48 sts).
Rnd 20: 48 dc (48 sts).
Rnd 21: (1 dc, dc2tog) 16 times (32 sts).
Rnd 22: (2 dc, dc2tog) 8 times (24 sts).
Rnd 23: (1 dc, dc2tog) 8 times (16 sts).
Stuff the Head firmly.
Cut the yarn and leave a long tail for sewing later.
With A, embroider a nose over 4 sts between rnds 15-16 in the centre of the face.
With black embroidery thread, embroider eyes over rnd 14.

BODY

Rnd 1: With B, working into MC, 8 dc (8 sts).
Rnd 2: (Dc2inc) 8 times (16 sts).
Rnd 3: (1 dc, dc2inc) 8 times (24 sts).
Rnd 4: 1 dc, dc2inc, (2 dc, dc2inc) 7 times, 1 dc (32 sts).
Rnd 5: (3 dc, dc2inc) 8 times (40 sts).
Rnd 6: Change to C. 2 dc, dc2inc, (4 dc, dc2inc) 7 times, 2 dc (48 sts).
Rnd 7: BLO 1 dc in each st around (48 sts).
Rnds 8 and 9: Change to B. 1 dc in each st around (48 sts).

Rnd 10: (10 dc, dc2tog) 4 times (44 sts).

Rnd 11: 1 dc in each st around (44 sts).

Rnds 12 and 13: 1 dc in each st around (44 sts).

Rnd 14: Change to D. 1 htr in each st around (44 sts).

Rnd 15: Change to B. 1 dc in each st around (44 sts).

Rnd 16: (9 dc, dc2tog) 4 times (40 sts).

Rnds 17 and 18: 1 dc in each st around (40 sts)

Rnd 19: (6 dc, dc2tog) 5 times (35 sts).

Rnd 20: 1 dc in each st around (35 sts).

Rnd 21: (5 dc, dc2tog) 5 times (30 sts).

Rnd 22: 1 dc in each st around (30 sts).

Rnd 23: (4 dc, dc2tog) 5 times (25 sts).

Rnd 24: 1 dc in each st around (25 sts).

Rnd 25: (3 dc, dc2tog) 5 times (20 sts).

Rnd 26: 1 dc in each st around (20 sts).

Rnd 27: (3 dc, dc2tog) 4 times (16 sts).

Cut the yarn and fasten off the yarn tail.

With E, embroider a gold detail on the belt.

Sew together the Body and the Head.

ARMS (MAKE 2)

Rnd 1: With A, working into MC, 8 dc (8 sts).

Rnds 2-4: 1 dc in each st around (8 sts).

Change to C.

Rnd 5: 1 dc in each st around (8 sts).

Change to B.

Rnd 6: BLO 1 dc in each st around (8 sts).

Rnds 7-16: 1 dc in each st around (8 sts).

Flatten the Arm, dc across into both sides to close the Arm.

Cut the yarn and leave a long tail for sewing later.

Cuff

With the hand pointing away from you, pull up a loop with C in the FLO from rnd 5. Dc in each loop around the Arm, sl st in first dc, cut yarn and fasten off the yarn tail.

Sew the Arms to the sides of the Body just under the Head.

BEARD

Row 1: With F and 4mm crochet hook, 13 ch, start in the second ch from the hook, 4 dc, 4 tr, 4 dc (12 sts).

Place and sew the Beard on to the Head.

HAT

Rnd 1: With C, 48 ch, sl st in first ch to make a circle. Make sure not to twist the chain (48 sts).

Rnd 2: 1 ch, start in the same st, 1 dc in each ch around, sl st in your first dc (48 sts).

Rnd 3: 1 ch, start in same st, 1 puff st (5 loops on hook) in each st around, sl st in first st, pull through with B (48 sts). Work in a spiral in continuous rnds from here.

Rnds 4-14: 1 dc in each st around (48 sts).

Rnd 15: 3 dc, dc2tog, (6 dc, dc2tog) 5 times, 3 dc (42 sts).

Rnds 16 and 17: 1 dc in each st around (42 sts).

Rnd 18: (5 dc, dc2tog) 6 times (36 sts).

Rnds 19 and 20: 1 dc in each st around (36 sts).

Rnd 21: 2 dc, dc2tog, (4 dc, dc2tog) 5 times, 2 dc (24 sts).

Rnds 22 and 23: 1 dc in each st around (24 sts).

Rnd 24: (3 dc, dc2tog) 6 times (24 sts).

Rnds 25 and 26: 1 dc in each st around (24 sts).

Rnd 27: 1 dc, dc2tog, (2 dc, dc2tog) 5 times, 1 dc (18 sts).

Rnds 28 and 29: 1 dc in each st around (18 sts).

Rnd 30: (1 dc, dc2tog) 6 times (12 sts).

Rnds 31 and 32: 1 dc in each st around (12 sts).

Rnd 33: (Dc2tog) 6 times (6 sts).

Cut the yarn and fasten off the yarn tail.

HAT DETAIL

With a 4mm crochet hook and E, working into MC, 6 dc (6 sts).

Cut the yarn and sew the circle on the end of the Hat.

Place and sew the Hat on to the Head.

Angel

A Christmas angel represents happiness, tranquillity and kindness, capturing the spirit of the holiday season by spreading love and warmth. With its peaceful presence and sweet smile, the Christmas angel reminds us to cherish small joys, display compassion and embrace the magic of this festive period.

SKILL LEVEL

FINISHED SIZE

4¾in (12cm)

SUPPLIES AND MATERIALS

Hobbii Rainbow Deluxe 8/4 100% Turkish cotton (approx 186yd/170m per 50g)

1 x 50g ball in 04 Winter White (A)

1 x 50g ball in 02 Natural White (B)

1 x 50g ball in 18 Light Malibu (C)

1 x 50g ball in 43 Pineapple (D)

Ricorumi Lamé DK 62% polyester, 38% polyamide (approx 55yd/50m per 10g)

1 x 10g ball in 002 Gold (E)

2mm (US B/1) crochet hook

Stitch marker (optional)

Darning needle

Polyester filling

Scissors

Black embroidery thread

PATTERN NOTE

The Angel is worked in continuous rounds unless otherwise stated.

BODY

Rnd 1: With C, working into MC, 8 dc (8 sts).
Rnd 2: (Dc2inc) 8 times (16 sts).
Rnd 3: (1 dc, dc2inc) 8 times (24 sts).
Rnd 4: 1 dc, dc2inc, (2 dc, dc2inc) 7 times, 1 dc (32 sts).
Rnd 5: (3 dc, dc2inc) 8 times (40 sts).
Rnd 6: 2 dc, dc2inc, (4 dc, dc2inc) 7 times, 2 dc (48 sts).
Rnd 7: BLO 1 dc in each st around (48 sts).
Rnds 8 and 9: 1 dc in each st around (48 sts).
Rnd 10: (10 dc, dc2tog) 4 times (44 sts).
Rnds 11-15: 1 dc in each st around (44 sts).
Rnd 16: (9 dc, dc2tog) 4 times (40 sts).
Rnds 17 and 18: 1 dc in each st around (40 sts).
Rnd 19: (6 dc, dc2tog) 5 times (35 sts).
Rnd 20: 1 dc in each st around (35 sts).
Rnd 21: (5 dc, dc2tog) 5 times (30 sts).
Rnd 22: 1 dc in each st around (30 sts).
Rnd 23: (4 dc, dc2tog) 5 times (25 sts).
Rnd 24: 1 dc in each st around (25 sts).
Rnd 25: (3 dc, dc2tog) 5 times (20 sts).
Rnd 26: 1 dc in each st around (20 sts).
Rnd 27: (3 dc, dc2tog) 4 times (16 sts).
Cut yarn and fasten off the yarn tail.
With E and the Angel's body pointing away from you, pull up a loop in the FLO from rnd 6, 1 dc in each st around (48 sts).
Cut yarn and fasten off the yarn tail.

HEAD

Rnd 1: With A, working into MC, 6 dc (6 sts).
Rnd 2: (Dc2inc) 6 times (12 sts).
Rnd 3: (1 dc, dc2inc) 6 times (18 sts).
Rnd 4: 1 dc, dc2inc, (2 dc, dc2inc) 5 times, 1 dc (24 sts).
Rnd 5: (3 dc, dc2inc) 6 times (30 sts).
Rnd 6: 2 dc, dc2inc, (4 dc, dc2inc) 5 times, 2 dc (36 sts).

Rnd 7: (5 dc, dc2inc) 6 times (42 sts).

Rnd 8: 3 dc, dc2inc, (6 dc, dc2inc) 5 times, 3 dc (48 sts).

Rnds 9-13: 1 dc in each st around (48 sts).

Rnd 14: (7 dc, dc2inc) 6 times (54 sts).

Rnds 15-18: 1 dc in each st around (54 sts).

Rnd 19: (7 dc, dc2tog) 6 times (48 sts).

Rnd 20: 1 dc in each st around (48 sts).

Rnd 21: (1 dc, dc2tog) 16 times (32 sts).

Rnd 22: (2 dc, dc2tog) 8 times (24 sts)

Rnd 23: (1 dc, dc2tog) 8 times (16 sts).

Stuff the Head firmly.

Cut yarn and leave a long tail for sewing later.

Sew together the Body and Head.

With A, embroider a nose between rnds 14 and 15.

With black embroidery thread, embroider eyes over rnd 13.

HAIR

Rnd 1: With D, working into MC, 6 dc (6 sts).

Rnd 2: (Dc2inc) 6 times (12 sts).

Rnd 3: (1 dc, dc2inc) 6 times (18 sts).

Rnd 4: 1 dc, dc2inc, (2 dc, dc2inc) 5 times, 1 dc (24 sts).

Rnd 5: (3 dc, dc2inc) 6 times (30 sts).

Rnd 6: 2 dc, dc2inc, (4 dc, dc2inc) 5 times, 2 dc (36 sts).

Rnd 7: (5 dc, dc2inc) 6 times (42 sts).

Rnd 8: 3 dc, dc2inc, (6 dc, dc2inc) 5 times, 3 dc (48 sts).

Rnd 9: (7 dc, dc2inc) 6 times (54 sts).

Rnds 10-12: 1 dc in each st around (54 sts).

Rnd 13: 16 dc, 4 htr, 3 tr, 1 htr, 1 sl st, 1 htr, 3 tr, 4 htr, 21 dc (54 sts).

Rnd 14: 24 dc, 1 sl st, 29 dc (54 sts).

Cut yarn and leave a long tail for sewing later.

Sew the Hair on the Head.

HAIR BUN

Rnd 1: With D, working into MC, 8 dc (8 sts).

Rnd 2: (Dc2inc) 8 times (16 sts).

Rnd 3: (1 dc, dc2inc) 8 times (24 sts).

Rnds 4-8: 1 dc in each st around (24 sts).

Cut yarn and leave a long tail for sewing later.

Sew the Hair Bun on top of the Head, stuff before closing the hole.

HEADBAND

With E, 26 ch, sl st into first ch to create a circle.

Place it on the Hair Bun, cut yarn, sew it securely.

ARMS (MAKE 2)

Rnd 1: With A, working into MC, 8 dc (8 sts).

Rnds 2-4: 1 dc in each st around (8 sts).

Change to C.

Rnds 5-16: 1 dc in each st around (8 sts).

Flatten the Arm, dc across into both sides to close the Arm.

Cut yarn and leave a long tail for sewing.

Place and sew the Arms just under the Head to the sides of the Body.

With A, sew together the hands.

WINGS (MAKE 2)

Row 1: With B, 6 ch, start in second ch from hook, 1 dc in next 4 sts, 1 sl st in the next st.

1 ch, turn (5 sts).

Row 2: Skip 1 st, 1 dc in the next 4 sts, 4 ch, turn your work (8 sts).

Row 3: Start in second ch from hook, 1 dc in the next 5 sts, dc2inc, 1 sl st. 1 ch, turn your work (8 sts).

Row 4: Skip 1 st, dc2inc, 1 dc in the next 6 sts, 4 ch, turn your work (12 sts)

Row 5: Start in second chain from hook, 1 dc in the next 10 sts, 1 sl st, 1 sl st in the 1 ch from the start (12 sts).

Cut yarn and leave a tail for sewing.

Place and sew on the Wings 5 rnds under the Head on the back, with 5 sts in between.

ORNAMENT OPTION

With E, add a loop on top of the Hair Bun to use the Angel as a tree decoration.

Christmas Elf

In the North Pole, Christmas elves work hard in Santa's workshop, crafting toys and spreading cheer.

SKILL LEVEL

FINISHED SIZE

5in (12.5cm)

SUPPLIES AND MATERIALS

Hobbii Rainbow Deluxe 8/4 100% Turkish cotton (approx 186yd/170m per 50g)

1 x 50g ball in 04 Winter White (A)

1 x 50g ball in 59 Apple Red (B)

1 x 50g ball in 02 Natural White (C)

1 x 50g ball in 39 Fern (D)

1 x 50g ball in 07 Chestnut (E)

1 x 50g ball in 09 Dark Chocolate (F)

Ricorumi Lamé DK 62% polyester, 38% polyamide (approx 55yd/50m per 10g)

1 x 10g ball in 002 Gold (G)

Black embroidery thread

2mm (US B/1) crochet hook

Stitch marker (optional)

Darning needle

Polyester filling

Scissors

Gold bell

HEAD

Rnd 1: With A, working into MC, 6 dc (6 sts).

Rnd 2: (Dc2inc) 6 times (12 sts).

Rnd 3: (1 dc, dc2inc) 6 times (18 sts).

Rnd 4: 1 dc, dc2inc, (2 dc, dc2inc) 5 times, 1 dc (24 sts).

Rnd 5: (3 dc, dc2inc) 6 times (30 sts).

Rnd 6: 2 dc, dc2inc, (4 dc, dc2inc) 5 times, 2 dc (36 sts).

Rnd 7: (5 dc, dc2inc) 6 times (42 sts).

Rnd 8: 3 dc, dc2inc, (6 dc, dc2inc) 5 times, 3 dc (48 sts).

Rnds 9-13: 1 dc in each st around (48 sts).

Rnd 14: (7 dc, dc2inc) 6 times (54 sts).

Rnds 15-18: 1 dc in each st around (54 sts).

Rnd 19: (7 dc, dc2tog) 6 times (48 sts).

Rnd 20: 1 dc in each st around (48 sts).

Rnd 21: (1 dc, dc2tog) 16 times (32 sts).

Rnd 22: (2 dc, dc2tog) 8 times (24 sts).

Rnd 23: (1 dc, dc2tog) 8 times (16 sts).

Stuff the Head firmly.

Cut yarn and leave a long tail for sewing later.

BODY

Rnd 1: With E, working into MC, 8 dc (8 sts).

Rnd 2: (Dc2inc) 8 times (16 sts).

Rnd 3: (1 dc, dc2inc) 8 times (24 sts).

Rnd 4: 1 dc, dc2inc, (2 dc, dc2inc) 7 times, 1 dc (32 sts).

Rnd 5: (3 dc, dc2inc) 8 times (40 sts).

Rnd 6: 2 dc, dc2inc, (4 dc, dc2inc) 7 times, 2 dc (48 sts).

Rnd 7: BLO 1 dc in each st around (48 sts).

Rnd 8: With B, 1 dc in each st around (48 sts).

Rnd 9: With C, 1 dc in each st around (48 sts).

Rnd 10: With B, (10 dc, dc2tog) 4 times (44 sts).

Rnd 11: With C, 1 dc in each st around (44 sts).

Rnd 12: With D, 1 dc in each st around (44 sts).

Rnd 13: BLO 1 dc in each st around (44 sts).

Rnd 14: With F, 1 htr in each st around (44 sts).

Rnd 15: With D, 1 dc in each st around (44 sts).

Rnd 16: (9 dc, dc2tog) 4 times (40 sts).

Rnds 17 and 18: 1 dc in each st around (40 sts)

Rnd 19: (6 dc, dc2tog) 5 times (35 sts).

Rnd 20: 1 dc in each st around (35 sts).

Rnd 21: (5 dc, dc2tog) 5 times (30 sts).

Rnd 22: 1 dc in each st around (30 sts).

Rnd 23: (4 dc, dc2tog) 5 times (25 sts).

Rnd 24: 1 dc in each st around (25 sts).

Rnd 25: (3 dc, dc2tog) 5 times (20 sts).

Rnd 26: 1 dc in each st around (20 sts).

Rnd 27: (3 dc, dc2tog) 4 times (16 sts).

Cut yarn and fasten off the yarn tail.

Sweater edge

With the Head facing you, pull up a loop with D in the FLO from rnd 12. 1 dc in each loop around, sl st in first dc, cut yarn and fasten off the yarn tail.

With G, embroider a gold detail on the belt (rnd 14 in F). Sew together the Body and Head.

ARMS (MAKE 2)

Rnd 1: With A, working into MC, 8 dc (8 sts).

Rnds 2-4: 1 dc in each st around (8 sts).

Rnds 5: With D, 1 dc in each st around (8 sts).

Rnd 6: BLO 1 dc in each st around (8 sts).

Rnds 7-16: 1 dc in each st around (8 sts).

Flatten the Arm, dc across into both sides to close the Arm. Cut yarn and leave a long tail for sewing later.

Arm edge

With the hand pointing away from you, pull up a loop with D in the FLO from rnd 5. 1 dc in each loop around the Arm, sl st in first dc, cut yarn and fasten off the yarn tail. Sew the Arms to the side of the Body just under the Head.

HAT

Rnd 1: With B, 48 ch, sl st in first ch to make a circle. Make sure not to twist the chain (48 sts).

Rnd 2: 1 ch, start in the same st. 1 dc in each ch around, sl st in your first dc (48 sts).

Work in a spiral in continuous rnds from here.

Rnd 3: With D, BLO 1 dc in each st around (48 sts).

Rnds 4-14: 1 dc in each st around (48 sts).

Rnd 15: 3 dc, dc2tog, (6 dc, dc2tog) 5 times, 3 dc (42 sts).

Rnds 16 and 17: 1 dc in each st around (42 sts).

Rnd 18: (5 dc, dc2tog) 6 times (36 sts).

Rnds 19 and 20: 1 dc in each st around (36 sts).

Rnd 21: 2 dc, dc2tog, (4 dc, dc2tog) 5 times, 2 dc (30 sts).

Rnds 22 and 23: 1 dc in each st around (30 sts).

Rnd 24: (3 dc, dc2tog) 6 times (24 sts).

Rnds 25 and 26: 1 dc in each st around (24 sts).

Rnd 27: 1 dc, dc2tog, (2 dc, dc2tog) 5 times, 1 dc (18 sts).

Rnds 28 and 29: 1 dc in each st around (18 sts).

Rnd 30: (1 dc, dc2tog) 6 times (12 sts).

Rnds 31 und 32: 1 dc in each st around (12 sts).

Rnd 33: (Dc2tog) 6 times (6 sts).

Cut yarn and close the hole using FLO. Sew on the gold bell at the top of the Hat. Fasten off the yarn tail.

Hat edge

Hold the Hat with the opening facing you. In B, pull up a loop at the back of the Hat in the FLO. (1 dc, 2 ch, sl st in your second ch, 1 dc in the next st) all the way around. Sl st in first dc.

Cut yarn and leave a long tail for sewing on the Hat.

FACE

With A, embroider a nose over 4 sts between rnds 15 and 16 in the centre of the Head.

Embroider eyes over rnd 14 using black embroidery thread.

Place and sew the Hat on to the Head.

Fold down the tip of the Hat to the side, secure with a few sts of same-coloured yarn.

EAR (RIGHT)

With A, working into MC, 3 dc, 3 tr, 3 ch, sl st. Pull tog the MC.

Cut yarn and sew the Ear to the right side of the Head in line with the embroidered face.

EAR (LEFT)

With A, working into MC 3 ch, 3 tr, 3 dc, sl st. Pull tog the MC.

Cut yarn and sew the Ear to the left side of the Head in line with the embroidered face.

Reindeer

Deck the halls with festive amigurumi cheer! This delightful crochet pattern guides you through creating a charming reindeer Christmas ornament. Perfect for crocheters of all skill levels, this project brings the magic of Santa's reindeer to your holiday décor.

SKILL LEVEL

●

FINISHED SIZE

4¾ x 2¾in (12 x 7cm)

SUPPLIES AND MATERIALS

Hobbii Friends Cotton 8/4 Mercerised 100% mercerised cotton (approx 174yd/160m per 50g)

1 x 50g ball in 009 Nougat (A)

1 x 50g ball in 001 White (B)

1 x 50g ball in 40 Tomato (C)

1 x 50g ball in 17 Cognac (D)

Black embroidery thread

2mm (US B/1) crochet hook

Darning needle

Polyester filling

Scissors

ORNAMENT OPTION

To make a loop for hanging the ornament, join A to the top of the Reindeer's Head with a sl st, dc in same st, then make as many ch as you like. I suggest you do that until you have a string of about 6in (15cm). Sl st in the last dc you made, fasten off, cut yarn and weave in the end.

HEAD

Rnd 1: With A, working into MC, 6 dc (6 sts).
Rnd 2: (Dc2inc) 6 times (12 sts).
Rnd 3: (1 dc, dc2inc) 6 times (18 sts).
Rnd 4: (2 dc, dc2inc) 6 times (24 sts).
Rnd 5: (3 dc, dc2inc) 6 times (30 sts).
Rnd 6: (4 dc, dc2inc) 6 times (36 sts).
Rnds 7-14: 1 dc in each st around (36 sts).
Rnd 15: (4 dc, dc2tog) 6 times (30 sts).
Rnd 16: (3 dc, dc2tog) 6 times (24 sts).
Rnd 17: (2 dc, dc2tog) 6 times (18 sts).
Stuff.
Fasten off, cut yarn and weave in the end.

BODY

Rnd 1: With A, working into MC, 6 dc (6 sts).
Rnd 2: (Dc2inc) 6 times (12 sts).
Rnd 3: (1 dc, dc2inc) 6 times (18 sts).
Rnd 4: (2 dc, dc2inc) 6 times (24 sts).
Rnd 5: (3 dc, dc2inc) 6 times (30 sts).
Rnd 6: (4 dc, dc2inc) 6 times (36 sts).
Rnd 7: (5 dc, dc2inc) 6 times (42 sts).
Rnd 8: (6 dc, dc2inc) 6 times (48 sts).
Rnds 9-18: 1 dc in each st around (48 sts).
Rnd 19: (6 dc, dc2tog) 6 times (42 sts).
Rnd 20: (5 dc, dc2tog) 6 times (36 sts).
Rnd 21: (4 dc, dc2tog) 6 times (30 sts).
Start stuffing.
Rnd 22: (3 dc, dc2tog) 6 times (24 sts).
Rnd 23: (2 dc, dc2tog) 6 times (18 sts).
Finish stuffing.
Fasten off, cut yarn and leave a long tail for sewing.
Sew together the Head and Body.

MUZZLE

Rnd 1: With B, working into MC, 6 dc (6 sts).
Rnd 2: (Dc2inc) 6 times (12 sts).
Rnd 3: (1 dc, dc2inc) 6 times (18 sts).
Rnds 4-6: 1 dc in each st around (18 sts).
Fasten off, cut yarn and leave a long tail for sewing.
Attach to the centre of the face, lower half towards the body, stuffing in the meantime.

NOSE

Rnd 1: With C, working into MC, 6 dc (6 sts).
Rnd 2: (1 dc, dc2inc) 3 times (9 sts).
Rnds 3 and 4: 1 dc in each st around (9 sts).
Rnd 5: (1 dc, dc2tog) 3 times (6 sts).
Fasten off, cut yarn and leave a long tail for sewing.
Weave the tail through the FLO on all 6 sts, pull to close and sew, a bit askew, on to the Muzzle. There is no need for stutting.

EARS (MAKE 2)

Rnd 1: With A, working into MC, 6 dc (6 sts).
Rnd 2: (1 dc, dc2inc) 3 times (9 sts).
Rnd 3: 1 dc in each st around (9 sts).
Rnd 4: (2 dc, dc2inc) 3 times (12 sts).
Rnd 5: 1 dc in each st around (12 sts).
Rnd 6: (2 dc, dc2tog) 3 times (9 sts).
Rnd 7: 1 dc in each st around (9 sts).
Fasten off, cut yarn and leave a long tail for sewing.
Sew the Ears to the Head, one on each side, leaving space for the Antlers. There is no need for stuffing.

LONG ANTLERS (MAKE 2)

Rnd 1: With D, working into MC, 6 dc (6 sts).
Rnd 2: (1 dc, dc2inc) 3 times (9 sts).
Rnd 3: 1 dc in each st around (9 sts).
Rnds 4-10: 1 dc in each st around (9 sts).
Fasten off, cut yarn and leave a long tail for sewing.
Sew the Long Antlers on to the Head, one on each side, between the Ears. There is no need for stuffing.

SHORT ANTLERS (MAKE 2)

Rnd 1: With D, working into MC, 6 dc (6 sts).
Rnd 2: 1 dc in each st around (6 sts).
Fasten off, cut yarn and leave a long tail for sewing.
Sew each Short Antler to the Long Antler, pointing towards the other Antler. There is no need for stuffing.

FINAL DETAILS

Embroider eyes on the Head with a piece of black embroidery thread. Embroider decorations on the belly and Head with B, using V-shaped stitches.

Snowman

Bring the magic of winter to your holiday decorations with this delightful crochet pattern for an amigurumi snowman ornament! This charming project is perfect for crocheters of all skill levels, making it a joy to create for yourself or as a heartfelt gift.

SKILL LEVEL

FINISHED SIZE

4¼ x 2½in (10.5 x 6cm)

SUPPLIES AND MATERIALS

Hobbii Friends Cotton 8/4 Mercerised 100% mercerised cotton (approx 174yd/160m per 50g)

1 x 50g ball in 001 White (A)

1 x 50g ball in 40 Tomato (B)

1 x 50g ball in 90 Capri Blue (C)

1 x 50g ball in 31 Pumpkin (D)

Black embroidery thread

2mm (US B/1) crochet hook

Darning needle

Polyester filling

Scissors

HEAD

Rnd 1: With A, working into MC, 6 dc (6 sts).
Rnd 2: (Dc2inc) 6 times (12 sts).
Rnd 3: (1 dc, dc2inc) 6 times (18 sts).
Rnd 4: (2 dc, dc2inc) 6 times (24 sts).
Rnd 5: (3 dc, dc2inc) 6 times (30 sts).
Rnd 6: (4 dc, dc2inc) 6 times (36 sts).
Rnds 7-14: 1 dc in each st around (36 sts).
Rnd 15: (4 dc, dc2dec) 6 times (30 sts).
Rnd 16: (3 dc, dc2dec) 6 times (24 sts).
Rnd 17: (2 dc, dc2dec) 6 times (18 sts).
Stuff.
Fasten off, cut yarn and weave in the end.

BODY

Rnd 1: With A, working into MC, 6 dc (6 sts).
Rnd 2: (Dc2inc) 6 times (12 sts).
Rnd 3: (1 dc, dc2inc) 6 times (18 sts).
Rnd 4: (2 dc, dc2inc) 6 times (24 sts).
Rnd 5: (3 dc, dc2inc) 6 times (30 sts).
Rnd 6: (4 dc, dc2inc) 6 times (36 sts).
Rnd 7: (5 dc, dc2inc) 6 times (42 sts).
Rnd 8: (6 dc, dc2inc) 6 times (48 sts).
Rnds 9-18: 1 dc in each st around (48 sts).
Rnd 19: (6 dc, dc2dec) 6 times (42 sts).
Rnd 20: (5 dc, dc2dec) 6 times (36 sts).
Rnd 21: (4 dc, dc2dec) 6 times (30 sts).
Start stuffing.
Rnd 22: (3 dc, dc2dec) 6 times (24 sts).
Rnd 23: (2 dc, dc2dec) 6 times (18 sts).
Finish stuffing.
Fasten off, cut yarn and leave a long tail for sewing.
Sew together the Head and Body.

NOSE

Rnd 1: With D, working into MC, 5 dc (5 sts).
Rnds 2 and 3: 1 dc in each st around (5 sts).
Rnd 4: 1 dc, dc2inc, 1 dc, dc2inc, 1 dc (7 sts).
Rnd 5: (Dc2inc) 7 times (14 sts).
Fasten off, cut yarn and leave a long tail for sewing.
There is no need to stuff. Sew Nose to centre of face.

HAT

Rnd 1: With B, working into MC, 6 dc (6 sts).
Rnd 2: (Dc2inc) 6 times (12 sts).
Rnd 3: (1 dc, dc2inc) 6 times (18 sts).
Rnd 4: (2 dc, dc2inc) 6 times (24 sts).
Rnd 5: BLO 24 dc (24 sts).
Rnds 6-9: 1 dc in each st around (24 sts).
Rnd 10: (FLO dc2inc) 24 times (48 sts).
Rnd 11: 48 dc, sl st to first dc (48 sts).
Fasten off, cut yarn and weave in the end.
Sew the Hat to the Head, a bit askew as shown
in the picture.
Embroider eyebrows, eyes and a mouth on the face
with a piece of black embroidery thread.

SCARF

Row 1: With C 71 ch, htr in second ch from the hook and in
all rem chs (70 sts).
Fasten off, cut yarn and weave in the end.
Wrap the Scarf around the Snowman's neck.

ORNAMENT OPTION

To make a loop for hanging the ornament: join A to the
top of the Snowman's Head with a sl st, dc in same st,
make as many ch as you like. I suggest you do that until
you have a string of about 6in (15cm), then sl st in the last
dc you made. Fasten off, cut yarn and weave in the end.

The Nutcracker

Spruce up your holiday décor with a touch of festive flair! This delightful amigurumi ornament crochet pattern lets you create miniature versions of these iconic Christmas-time soldiers. Feeling creative? Personalise your nutcrackers with different yarn colours or add a tiny sword for an extra touch of holiday spirit.

SKILL LEVEL

●

FINISHED SIZE

8 x 2½in (20 x 6cm)

SUPPLIES AND MATERIALS

Hobbii Friends Cotton 8/4 Mercerised 100% mercerised cotton (approx 174yd/160m per 50g)

1 x 50g ball in 124 Black (A)

1 x 50g ball in 40 Tomato (B)

1 x 50g ball in 009 Nougat (C)

1 x 50g ball in 001 White (D)

1 x 50g ball in 24 Sunflower (E)

2mm (US B/1) crochet hook

Darning needle

Polyester filling

Scissors

ORNAMENT OPTION

Join whichever colour yarn you prefer to the top centre of the Hat with a (sl st, 1 ch, 1 dc) in same dc, then proceed with making as many ch as you like. I suggest you do that until you have a string of about 6in (15cm). Sl st in the last dc you made, fasten off, cut and weave in the end.

BODY

Rnd 1: With A, working into MC, 8 dc (8 sts).
Rnd 2: (Dc2inc) 8 times (16 sts).
Rnd 3: (1 dc, dc2inc) 8 times (24 sts).
Rnd 4: (2 dc, dc2inc) 8 times (32 sts).
Rnd 5: (3 dc, dc2inc) 8 times (40 sts).
Rnd 6: (4 dc, dc2inc) 8 times (48 sts).
Rnd 7: BLO 1 dc in each st around (48 sts).
Rnds 8-11: 1 dc in each st around (48 sts).
Change to E.
Rnds 12 and 13: 1 dc in each st around (48 sts).
Change to B.
Rnds 14-19: 1 dc in each st around (48 sts).
Change to E.
Rnds 20 and 21: 1 dc in each st around (48 sts).
Change to B.
Rnds 22-31: 1 dc in each st around (48 sts).
Start stuffing.
Rnd 32: (4 dc, dc2tog) 8 times (40 sts)
Rnd 33: (8 dc, dc2tog) 4 times (36 sts).
Rnd 34: (4 dc, dc2tog) 6 times (30 sts).
Rnd 35: (3 dc, dc2tog) 6 times (24 sts).
Change to C.
Rnd 36: (1 dc, dc2tog) 8 times (16 sts).
Rnd 37: 1 dc in each st around (16 sts).
Fasten off, cut yarn leaving a long tail for sewing.
Finish stuffing the Body.

HAT AND HEAD

Rnd 1: With A, working into MC, 8 dc (8 sts.)
Rnd 2: (Dc2inc) 8 times (16 sts).
Rnd 3: (1 dc, dc2inc) 8 times (24 sts).
Rnd 4: (2 dc, dc2inc) 8 times (32 sts).
Rnd 5: (3 dc, dc2inc) 8 times (40 sts).
Rnd 6: (4 dc, dc2inc) 8 times (48 sts).
Rnd 7: BLO 1 dc in each st around (48 sts).
Rnds 8-12: 1 dc in each st around (48 sts).
Change to E.
Rnds 13 and 14: 1 dc in each st around (48 sts).
Change to A.
Rnds 15-31: 1 dc in each st around (48 sts).
Change to C.

Rnd 32: BLO (4 dc, dc2tog) 8 times (40 sts).
Rnds 33-38: 1 dc in each st around (40 sts).
Start stuffing.
Rnd 39: (3 dc, dc2tog) 8 times (32 sts).
Rnd 40: (2 dc, dc2tog) 8 times (24 sts).
Rnd 41: (1 dc, dc2tog) 8 times (16 sts).
Finish stuffing.
Fasten off, cut yarn and weave in the end.
With the Hat and Head upside down, join B to the FLO
of a st of rnd 31 with a sl st, 1 ch, htr in same st and all
rem sts of rnd, sl st to first htr made (48 sts).
Fasten off, cut yarn and weave in end.
Sew together the Head and Body.

MOUSTACHE

Row 1: With D, 16 ch, dc in second st from the hook,
dc in next 2 sts, 1 htr, 1 tr, 1 htr, 1 dc in next 3 sts, 1 htr, 1 tr, 1 htr,
1 dc in last 3 sts, turn (15 sts).
Row 2: 1 ch, sl st in first st and in next 2 sts, 1 htr, 1 tr, 1 htr,
sl st in next 3 sts, 1 htr, 1 tr, 1 htr, sl st in last 3 sts, fasten off,
cut and weave in the end (15 sts).
Sew the Mustache to the face, under the Hat, fixing
the middle of the Mustache to the middle of the face,
balanced between the Hat and the neck joining with
the Body. For this Nutcracker, there will be no eyes
added to the face.
With E, embroider the front part of the shirt with
4 'X' shapes, as shown in the pictures.

SHORT HAIR (MAKE 2)

Row 1: With D, 21 ch, 2 dc in second ch from the hook
and in all rem ch, turn (40 sts).
Fasten off, cut yarn and leave a long tail for sewing.

LONG HAIR (MAKE 2)

Row 1: With D, 26 ch, 2 dc in second ch from the hook
and in all rem ch, turn (50 sts).
Fasten off, cut yarn and leave a long tail for sewing.
Sew one Long and one Short piece of Hair on to each
side of the Head, the first one behind the second one,
right under the Hat's brim.

Polar Bear

Magnificent Polar bears capture the essence of Christmas. This one is keeping toasty warm in a sunny yellow scarf, perfect for your Christmas tree.

SKILL LEVEL

FINISHED SIZE
4in (10cm)

SUPPLIES AND MATERIALS
Hobbii Rainbow Deluxe 8/4 100% Turkish cotton (approx 186yd/170m per 50g)

1 x 50g ball in 001 White (A)

1 x 50g ball in 55 Sunny Yellow (B)

Silver or gold crochet thread

Stitch markers

Darning needle

Polyester filling

Scissors

Sewing pins

PATTERN NOTES

The Polar Bear pieces are worked in rounds and the Scarf is worked in rows. When turning at the end of a row, place the first htr in the second st from the hook.

HEAD

Note: Stuff as you crochet.
Rnd 1: With A, working into MC, 6 dc (6 sts).
Rnd 2: (Dc2inc) 6 times (12 sts).
Rnd 3: (Dc, dc2inc) 6 times (18 sts).
Rnd 4: (Dc, dc2inc, dc) 6 times (24 sts).
Rnd 5: (3 dc, dc2inc) 6 times (30 sts).
Rnd 6: (2 dc, dc2inc, 2 dc) 6 times (36 sts).
Rnd 7: (5 dc, dc2inc) 6 times (42 sts).
Rnd 8: (3 dc, dc2inc, 3 dc) 6 times (48 sts).
Rnds 9-14: 1 dc in each st around (48 sts).
Rnd 15: (3 dc, dc2tog, 3 dc) 6 times (42 sts).
Rnds 16 and 17: 1 dc in each st around (42 sts).
Rnd 18: (5 dc, dc2tog) 6 times (36 sts).
Rnds 19 and 20: 1 dc in each st around (36 sts).
Rnd 21: (2 dc, dc2tog, 2 dc) 6 times (30 sts).
Rnd 22: 1 dc in each st around (30 sts).

Rnd 23: (3 dc, dc2tog) 6 times (24 sts).
Rnd 24: (Dc, dc2tog, dc) 6 times (18 sts).
Rnd 25: (Dc, dc2tog) 6 times (12 sts).
Rnd 26: (Dc, dc2tog) 4 times (8 sts).
Fasten off and leave a long yarn tail for attaching later.

NOSE

Note: Do not stuff. Stuffing will be added later when assembling the pieces.
Rnd 1: With A, working into MC, 6 dc (6 sts).
Rnd 2: (Dc2inc) 6 times (12 sts).
Rnd 3: (Dc, dc2inc) 6 times (18 sts).
Rnd 4: 1 dc in each st around (18 sts).
Fasten off and leave a long tail for attaching.

EARS (MAKE 2)

Rnd 1: With A, working into MC, 2 ch, 9 tr (11 sts).
Pull the MC yarn end to close the MC, but do not fasten off the last tr to the 2nd ch, leave it in the shape of a half circle. Leave a long tail for attaching.

BODY

Note: Stuff as you crochet.
Rnd 1: With A, working into MC, 6 dc (6 sts).
Rnd 2: (Dc2inc) 6 times (12 sts).
Rnd 3: (Dc, dc2inc) 6 times (18 sts).
Rnd 4: (Dc, dc2inc, dc) 6 times (24 sts).
Rnd 5: (3 dc, dc2inc) 6 times (30 sts).
Rnd 6: (2 dc, dc2inc, 2 dc) 6 times (36 sts).
Rnd 7: 1 dc in each st around (36 sts).
Rnd 8: (5 dc, dc2inc) 6 times (42 sts).
Rnds 9-11: 1 dc in each st around (42 sts).
Rnd 12: (3 dc, dc2inc, 3 dc) 6 times (48 sts).
Rnds 13-16: 1 dc in each st around (48 sts).
Rnd 17: (3 dc, dc2tog, 3 dc) 6 times (42 sts).
Rnds 18 and 19: 1 dc in each st around (42 sts).
Rnd 20: (5 dc, dc2tog) 6 times (36 sts).
Rnd 21: 1 dc in each st around (36 sts).
Rnd 22: (2 dc, dc2tog, 2 dc) 6 times (30 sts).
Rnd 23: (3 dc, dc2tog) 6 times (24 sts).
Rnd 24: 1 dc in each st around (24 sts).
Fasten off and leave a long yarn tail for attaching later.

ARMS (MAKE 2)

Note: Lightly stuff as you crochet, but only up to rnd 8.
Rnd 1: With A, working into MC, 6 dc (6 sts).
Rnd 2: (Dc2inc) 6 times (12 sts).
Rnds 3-14: 1 dc in each st around (12 sts).
Pinch the Arms closed, dc through both sides with 6 dc and close the opening (6 sts).
Fasten off and leaving a long tail for attaching.

SCARF

Row 1: With B, 6 ch, turn (6 sts).
Row 2: 5 htr, 1 ch, turn (6 sts).
Rows 3-70: Htr in each st along (6 sts).
Fasten off and weave in the yarn ends.

ASSEMBLY

Pin the Ears to the side of the Head starting between rnds 17 and 18 and ending around 22 and 23, evenly spaced on the Head. When they are pinned evenly, whip stitch them on using the darning needle and the leftover yarn ends from the Ears. Weave the extra tails into the Head.

Using pins, secure the Nose to the front of the face centred between the two Ears, with the bottom of the Nose at rnd 7 and the top at rnd 14 of the Head. With the darning needle and the leftover yarn tail, whip stitch around the Nose until it is sewn in place. Before closing the last 4 whip stitches, add a small amount of stuffing to the Nose. Once finished, hide the yarn end within the Head.

Before attaching the Head to the Body, use pins to ensure the placement is correct. Match up rnd 4 of the Head and rnd 24 of the Body, having 24 sts each. Once aligned and centred, whip stitch the two pieces together using the darning needle and the long tail left over from the Body. When finished, weave in the end.

The Arms should be pinned 1 rnd down from the Head on the sides of the Body. Leave at least 8 sts between them on the front of the Body and angle them slightly forward.

If they are even, you can start whip stitching the top seam of the Arms to the Body using the darning needle and the leftover yarn ends. If not, take this time to adjust the Arms up or down, to ensure a good placement. Then add two or three extra whip stitches to the back of each of the Arms near the seams to keep them steady. When complete, secure and weave in the ends.

Use six pins to mark where the eyes will be added, with each eye starting at rnd 14 of the Head in a triangle shape. The first pin for the eye should be 2 sts away from the top of the Nose and the second 4 sts away. Then add the third pin 1 rnd above and centred between the two eye pins. Repeat for the second eye.

To embroider the eyes, use crochet thread in black and the darning needle, enter at the side of the Head, exit at the first pin, then enter the stitch at the second pin. To make the triangle shape, bring the needle up to the third pin, loop the needle around the thread, and enter through the same stitch. This circles the thread to make the shape and holds it in place. Exit the needle through the side of the Head where you entered, tie the ends and hide them in the Head.

Put a pin in the centre of the Nose between rnds 2 and 3. With the darning needle, enter the yarn through the bottom of the Head and 1 st to the side of the Nose pin. Whip stitch a little black detail on the Nose about 10 times and 3 sts long; with the pin centred, the whip stitch will enter and exit 1 st on either side of where the pin is located. Once complete, exit the yarn back through the same stitch on the bottom of the head, knot the two ends and wrap the Scarf around the neck twice.

ORNAMENT OPTION

To make a loop to hang the ornament, thread a darning needle with either silver or gold crochet thread. Enter the needle on the right side of the magic circle and exit on the left side of the magic circle. Tie the two yarn ends together to complete the loop.

Tasty treats

Christmas Pudding

Sweeten up your Christmas with this traditional festive dessert.

SKILL LEVEL

FINISHED SIZE

2½in (6cm)

SUPPLIES AND MATERIALS

Hobbii Rainbow Deluxe 8/4 100% Turkish cotton (approx 186yd/170m per 50g)

1 x 50g ball in 07 Mahogany (A)

1 x 50g ball in 02 Natural White (B)

1 x 50g ball in 59 Apple Red (C)

Hobbii Rainbow 8/4 100% cotton (approx 174yd/160m per 50g)

1 x 50g ball in 99 Malachite (D)

2mm (US B/1) crochet hook

Stitch marker (optional)

Darning needle

Polyester filling

Scissors

PUDDING

Rnd 1: With A, working into MC, 6 dc (6 sts).
Rnd 2: (Dc2inc) 6 times (12 sts).
Rnd 3: (1 dc, dc2inc) 6 times (18 sts).
Rnd 4: 1 dc, dc2inc, (2 dc, dc2inc) 5 times, 1 dc (24 sts).
Rnd 5: (3 dc, dc2inc) 6 times (30 sts).
Rnd 6: 2 dc, dc2inc, (4 dc, dc2inc) 5 times, 2 dc (36 sts).
Rnd 7: (5 dc, dc2inc) 6 times (42 sts).
Rnd 8: 3 dc, dc2inc, (6 dc, dc2inc) 5 times, 3 dc (48 sts).
Rnds 9-17: 1 dc in each st around (48 sts).
Rnd 18: 3 dc, dc2tog, (6 dc, dc2tog) 5 times, 3 dc (42 sts).
Rnd 19: (5 dc, dc2tog) 6 times (36 sts).
Rnd 20: Work this rnd in the BLO: 2 dc, dc2tog, (4 dc, dc2tog) 4 times, 2 dc (30 sts).
Rnd 21: (3 dc, dc2tog) 6 times (24 sts).
Rnd 22: 1 dc, dc2tog, (2 dc, dc2tog) 5 times, 1 dc (18 sts).
Rnd 23: (1 dc, dc2tog) 6 times (12 sts).
Stuff the Pudding firmly.
Rnd 24: (Dc2tog) 6 times. (6 sts).
Cut yarn, close the hole using the FLO and fasten off the yarn tail.

ICING

Rnd 1: With B, working into MC, 6 dc (6 sts).
Rnd 2: (Dc2inc) 6 times (12 sts).
Rnd 3: (1 dc, dc2inc) 6 times (18 sts).
Rnd 4: 1 dc, dc2inc, (2 dc, dc2inc) 5 times, 1 dc (24 sts).
Rnd 5: (3 dc, dc2inc) 6 times (30 sts).
Rnd 6: 2 dc, dc2inc, (4 dc, dc2inc) 5 times, 2 dc (36 sts).
Rnd 7: (5 dc, dc2inc) 6 times (42 sts).
Rnd 8: 3 dc, dc2inc, (6 dc, dc2inc) 5 times, 3 dc (48 sts).
Rnd 9: (Skip 1 st, 5 tr all in next st, skip 1 st, sl st) 12 times (48 sts).
Cut yarn and leave a long tail for sewing.

HOLLY BERRIES (MAKE 2)

Rnd 1: With C, working into MC, 7 dc (7 sts).
Rnds 2 and 3: 1 dc in each st around (7 sts).
Sl st in the next st.
Stuff lightly.
Cut yarn and leave a long tail for sewing.

LEAVES (MAKE 2)

Rnd 1: With D, 10 ch. Start in the second ch from the hook, 1 dc, 2 htr, 1 tr, 2 tr in next st, 1 tr, 2 htr, 1 dc. Turn and work on the other side of the ch. 1 dc, 2 htr, 1 tr, 2 tr in next st, 1 tr, 2 htr, 1 dc (20 sts).
Rnd 2: (Htr, 2 ch, sl st in the second ch from the hook, 1 htr in the same st, 2 sl st) 6 times. 1 htr, 2 ch, sl st in the second ch from your hook, htr in the same st, 1 sl st, 4 ch, start in the second ch from the hook and make 3 sl st back.
Cut yarn and leave a tail for sewing.

ASSEMBLY

Place and whip stitch the Icing on top of the Pudding using the darning needle. Then place and whip stitch the Leaves and the Holly Berries on top of the Icing.
Using a darning needle and either gold or silver crochet thread, add a loop at the top of the ornament so it can hang on the Christmas tree.

Hot Chocolate

During the festive period, a cup of Christmas hot cocoa
topped with fluffy marshmallows is like a hug in a mug!

SKILL LEVEL

FINISHED SIZE

2½in (6cm)

SUPPLIES AND MATERIALS

Hobbii Rainbow Deluxe 8/4 100% Turkish cotton (approx 186yd/170m per 50g)

1 x 50g ball in 39 Fern (A)

1 x 50g ball in 09 Dark Chocolate (B)

1 x 50g ball in 02 Natural White (C)

Rico Creative Chenillove 100% polyester (approx 120yd/110m per 100g)

Small amount in 01 Cream (D)

Ricorumi Lamé DK 62% polyester, 38% polyamide (approx 55yd/50m per 10g)

1 x 10g ball in 02 Gold (E)

2mm (US B/1) crochet hook

Stitch marker (optional)

Darning needle

Polyester filling

Scissors

Cardboard (optional)

Pipe cleaner (optional)

CHOCOLATE

Rnd 1: With B, working into MC, 6 dc (6 sts).

Rnd 2: (Dc2inc) 6 times (12 sts).

Rnd 3: (1 dc, dc2inc) 6 times (18 sts).

Rnd 4: 1 dc, dc2inc, (2 dc, dc2inc) 5 times, 1 dc (24 sts).

Rnd 5: (3 dc, dc2inc) 6 times (30 sts).

Rnd 6: 2 dc, dc2inc, (4 dc, dc2inc) 5 times, 2 dc (36 sts).

Rnd 7: (5 dc, dc2inc) 6 times (42 sts).

Sl st in the next st, cut yarn and fasten off the yarn end.

With D, embroider marshmallows.

MUG

Rnd 1: With A, working into MC, 6 dc (6 sts).

Rnd 2: (Dc2inc) 6 times (12 sts).

Rnd 3: (1 dc, dc2inc) 6 times (18 sts).

Rnd 4: 1 dc, dc2inc, (2 dc, dc2inc) 5 times, 1 dc (24 sts).

Rnd 5: (3 dc, dc2inc) 6 times (30 sts).

Rnd 6: 2 dc, dc2inc, (4 dc, dc2inc) 5 times, 2 dc (36 sts).

Rnd 7: (5 dc, dc2inc) 6 times (42 sts).

Rnd 8: BLO 1 dc in each st around (42 sts).

Cut out a round circle of cardboard that fits in the bottom of the Mug.

Rnds 9-21: 1 dc in each st around (42 sts).

Rnd 22: Add the Chocolate on top of the Mug.

Through both parts, 1 dc in each st around.

Stuff firmly before closing the hole (42 sts).

Rnd 23: With C, FLO 1 dc in each st around (42 sts).

Cut yarn and fasten off the yarn end.

With E, embroider a snowflake on the Mug between rnds 9 and 19.

HANDLE

Rnd 1: With A, working into MC, 6 dc (6 sts).

Rnds 2-14: 1 dc in each st around (6 sts).

Sl st in the next st, cut yarn and leave a long tail for sewing.

Stuff the Handle lightly or add a pipe cleaner in the Handle so you can shape it.

Sew on the Handle over rnds 8 and 9 and 19 and 20 of the Mug.

ORNAMENT OPTION

With E, add a loop at the top of the Hot Chocolate mug so it can hang on the Christmas tree.

Gingerbread Man

Fill your holidays with the sweet scent of nostalgia! This charming amigurumi pattern lets you create adorable miniature gingerbread men to adorn your Christmas tree. Perfect for beginners and experienced crocheters alike.

SKILL LEVEL

FINISHED SIZE

4¼ x 2½in (11 x 6.5cm)

SUPPLIES AND MATERIALS

Hobbii Friends Cotton 8/4 Mercerised 100% mercerised cotton (approx 174yd/160m per 50g)

1 x 50g ball in 009 Nougat (A)

1 x 50g ball in 40 Tomato (B)

1 x 50g ball in 001 White (C)

Black and red embroidery thread

2mm (US B/1) crochet hook

Darning needle

Polyester filling

Scissors

HEAD
Rnd 1: With A, working into MC, 6 dc (6 sts).
Rnd 2: (Dc2inc) 6 times (12 sts).
Rnd 3: (1 dc, dc2inc) 6 times (18 sts).
Rnd 4: (2 dc, dc2inc) 6 times (24 sts).
Rnd 5: (3 dc, dc2inc) 6 times (30 sts).
Rnd 6: (4 dc, dc2inc) 6 times (36 sts).
Rnds 7-14: 1 dc in each st around (36 sts).
Rnd 15: (4 dc, dc2tog) 6 times (30 sts).
Rnd 16: (3 dc, dc2tog) 6 times (24 sts).
Rnd 17: (2 dc, dc2tog) 6 times (18 sts).
Stuff.
Fasten off, cut yarn and weave in the yarn ends.

BODY
Rnd 1: With A, working into MC, 6 dc (6 sts).
Rnd 2: (Dc2inc) 6 times (12 sts).
Rnd 3: (1 dc, dc2inc) 6 times (18 sts).
Rnd 4: (2 dc, dc2inc) 6 times (24 sts).
Rnd 5: (3 dc, dc2inc) 6 times (30 sts).
Rnd 6: (4 dc, dc2inc) 6 times (36 sts).
Rnd 7: (5 dc, dc2inc) 6 times (42 sts).
Rnd 8: (6 dc, dc2inc) 6 times (48 sts).
Rnds 9 and 10: 1 dc in each st around (48 sts).
Change to B.
Rnds 11 and 12: 1 dc in each st around (48 sts).
Change to C.
Rnds 13 and 14: 1 dc in each st around (48 sts).
Change to A.
Rnds 15-18: 1 dc in each st around (48 sts).
Rnd 19: (6 dc, dc2tog) 6 times (42 sts).
Rnd 20: (5 dc, dc2tog) 6 times (36 sts).
Rnd 21: (4 dc, dc2tog) 6 times (30 sts).
Start stuffing.
Rnd 22: (3 dc, dc2tog) 6 times (24 sts).
Rnd 23: (2 dc, dc2tog) 6 times (18 sts).
Finish stuffing.
Fasten off, cut yarn and leave a long tail for sewing.
Sew the Head and Body together.

ICING
Rnd 1: With C, working into MC, 6 dc (6 sts).
Rnd 2: (Dc2inc) 6 times (12 sts).
Rnd 3: (1 dc, dc2inc) 6 times (18 sts).
Rnd 4: (2 dc, dc2inc) 6 times (24 sts).
Rnd 5: (Sl st, 3 htr) 6 times (24 sts).
Rnd 6: *Sl st, (2 tr in next st) 3 times; rep from * 5 more times (42 sts).
Rnd 7: *2 sl st, htr, (2 tr in next st) twice, htr, sl st; rep from * 5 more times (54 sts).
Fasten off, cut yarn and leave a long tail for sewing.
Sew the Icing to the top of the Head.

BOW TIE
With B, 4 ch.
Row 1: Dc in second ch from hook and in all rem ch, turn (3 sts).
Rows 2 and 3: 1 ch, dc in first and in all rem sts, turn (3 sts).
Row 4: 1 ch, dc2tog in first st, dc in next st, turn (2 sts).
Rows 5-7: Rep row 2 (2 sts).
Row 8: 1 ch, dc2inc in first st, dc in next st, turn (3 sts).
Rows 9-11: Rep row 2 (3 sts).
Fasten off, cut yarn and weave in the yarn end.
Wrap a bit of yarn around the middle of the Bow Tie, then sew it to the centre of the Body, underneath the Head.

ASSEMBLY
With black thread, embroider the eyes and mouth.
With red thread, embroider the cheeks.

ORNAMENT OPTION
To make a loop for hanging the ornament, join A to the top of the Gingerbread Man's Head with a sl st, dc in same st, then make as many ch as you like. I suggest you do that until you have a string of about 6in (15cm). Sl st in the last dc you made, fasten off, cut yarn and weave in the yarn end.

Slice of Christmas Cake

Spruce up your Christmas tree with a slice of pure sweetness!
This whimsical amigurumi pattern lets you whip up adorable miniature cakes
to adorn your holiday décor. Choose festive colours for the cake layers and frosting,
add sprinkles or a cherry on top, and personalise these charming ornaments
to reflect your favourite holiday treats.

SKILL LEVEL

FINISHED SIZE
3¼ x 3¼in (8.5 x 8.5cm)

SUPPLIES AND MATERIALS
Hobbii Friends Cotton 8/4 Mercerised 100% mercerised cotton (approx 174yd/160m per 50g)
1 x 50g ball in 17 Cognac (A)
1 x 50g ball in 24 Sunflower (B)
1 x 50g ball in 01 White (C)
Small amount of various colours for sugar sprinkles
2mm (US B/1) crochet hook
Darning needle
Polyester filling
Scissors

PATTERN NOTE

Make six identical Cake Sides: four squares using A only and two squares using B, with stripes of A in rows 7, 8-14 and 15.

While working on your pieces, there won't be an actual RS or WS, since the sts look the same on both sides.

CAKE SIDE (MAKE 6: 4 IN A AND 2 IN B WITH A STRIPES)

Row 1: 21 ch, 1 dc in second ch from the hook and in all rem sts, turn (20 sts).

Row 2: 1 ch, 1 dc in first and in all remaining sts, turn. (20 sts).

Rows 3-21: Rep row 2 (20 sts).

Fasten off, cut yarn and weave in the tail.

Your piece should be a square and meas around 2¾in (7.2cm) per side. If you need to, in order to get a square shape, you can add or subtract rows with the same pattern rep as above. Furthermore, if you wish to make a bigger or smaller Cake, add more or fewer sts per row and more or fewer rows per square.

ASSEMBLY

You can now join all six identical Cake Sides together in order to create a cube. When you are almost done and have around 10 sts left to join on your last side, fill the Cake with stuffing before finishing the last joining sts.

Use A for joining A squares together, B for joining B squares, and A again when joining A squares to B squares. The top, bottom and two adjacent Sides will be in A, with the two opposite sides in B, as pictured left. On the side where the two B Sides are joined, if you prefer, you can use B for joining all B rows, and A for A rows, otherwise just B is also good.

Start by placing two Cake Sides one on top of the other, wrong sides facing each other.

Join the indicated colour with a sl st to any corner st. Every corner st will always have a dc, a 1 ch space and another dc on the next side.

(1 ch, 1 dc) in same st and all rem sts (you should place 1 dc in each row end) to the last st, going through both pieces.

1 ch, do not work on your second Side anymore, instead place your third Side.

Join the first and third pieces: 1 dc in same st as the previous dc on the first piece, going through the corresponding first st of the third Side before that, then dc in all remaining sts on that side to the last one, through both layers.

1 ch, then rep the same steps for the fourth and fifth Sides. This way, your first Side will be joined on all four sides to the other four Sides. Fasten off, cut yarn and weave in the end.

Join the opposite sides of pieces 2, 3, 4 and 5 from the ones already joined, to each side of piece 6. Remember to always work through two layers, putting (1 dc, 1 ch, 1 dc) in each corner. Fasten off, cut yarn and weave in the end.

To join the remaining four sides of the cube, as before, dc in all sts of each side, but this time there is no need to place 1 ch in the corners – simply fasten off, cut yarn and weave in the ends each time.

CRUST

Looking at the Cake from behind, join A to the top right corner with a sl st, 1 ch, 1 dc in same st and in all rem sts on first and then on second side until last corner, turn.
1 ch, 3 htr in first and all remaining sts.

Fasten off, cut yarn and weave in the tail.
Add the Crust to the two top sides of the Cake where only A squares are joined.

WHIPPED CREAM

Row 1: With C, 36 ch, 2 dc in second ch from the hook and in all rem sts, turn (75 sts).
Row 2: 2 tr in first and all rem sts (150 sts).
Fasten off and cut yarn, leaving a long tail for sewing. Roll the Whipped Cream around to make a rose shape and sew it to the centre of the top of your Cake.

SPRINKLES (OPTIONAL)

If you like, you can embroider the top of your Cake with coloured sugar sprinkles, using multiple colours of yarn, as shown in the picture.

ORNAMENT OPTION

To make a loop for hanging the ornament, join A to the corner of the cube where the two sides with Crust meet, with a sl st, dc in same st, then make as many ch as you like. I suggest you do that until you have a string of about 6in (15cm). Sl st in the last dc, fasten off, cut yarn and weave in the end.

Brussels Sprout

Love them or hate them, these tiny green vegetables are a Christmas dinner staple.
Whether you're a fan or not, there's no denying that the Brussels sprout
adds a touch of tradition and nostalgia to any holiday meal.

SKILL LEVEL

●

FINISHED SIZE

2 x 2in (5 x 5cm)

SUPPLIES AND MATERIALS

Hobbii Rainbow Deluxe 8/4 100% Turkish cotton (approx 186yd/170m per 50g)

1 x 50g ball in 39 Fern (A)

1 x 50g ball in 38 Crocodile (B)

Silver or gold crochet thread

2mm (US B/1) crochet hook

Darning needle

Polyester filling

Scissors

Stitch markers

Sewing pins

PATTERN NOTE

Stuff the Brussels Sprout as you crochet.

BRUSSELS SPROUT

Rnd 1: With A, working into MC, 6 dc (6 sts).
Rnd 2: (Dc2inc) 6 times (12 sts).
Rnd 3: (Dc, dc2inc) 6 times (18 sts).
Rnd 4: (Dc, dc2inc, dc) 6 times (24 sts).
Rnd 5: (3 dc, dc2inc) 6 times (30 sts).
Rnd 6: 1 dc in each st around (30 sts).
Rnd 7: (2 dc, dc2inc, 2 dc) 6 times (36 sts).
Rnd 8: 1 dc in each st around (36 sts).
Rnd 9: (5 dc, dc2inc) 6 times (42 sts).
Rnds 10-13: 1 dc in each st around (42 sts).
Rnd 14: (5 dc, dc2tog) 6 times (36 sts).
Rnd 15: 1 dc in each st around (36 sts).
Rnd 16: (2 dc, dc2tog, 2 dc) 6 times (30 sts).
Rnd 17: 1 dc in each st around (30 sts).
Rnd 18: (3 dc, dc2tog) 6 times (24 sts).
Rnd 19: (Dc, dc2tog, dc) 6 times (18 sts).
Rnd 20: (Dc, dc2tog) 6 times (12 sts).
Rnd 21: (Dc, dc2tog) 4 times (8 sts).
Fasten off and weave the yarn under each of the FLO, then pull tight and hide the yarn end in the Brussels Sprout.

SPROUT LEAVES (MAKE 3)

Rnd 1: With B, working into MC, 6 dc (6 sts).
Rnd 2: (Dc2inc) 6 times (12 sts).
Rnd 3: (Dc, dc2inc) 6 times (18 sts).
Rnd 4: (Dc, dc2inc, dc) 6 times (24 sts).
Rnd 5: (3 dc, dc2inc) 6 times (30 sts).
Rnd 6: (2 dc, dc2inc, 2 dc) 6 times (36 sts).
Rnds 7-9: 1 dc in each st around (36 sts).
Rnd 10: (5 dc, dc2inc) twice, (5 htr, htr2inc) twice, (5 dc, dc2inc) twice (42 sts).
Fasten off and leave a long tail for attaching.

ASSEMBLY

Place one of the Leaves on the side of the Brussels Sprout with the htrs pointing upwards and the last stitch of the Leaf, overlapping rnd 21 of the Sprout, and pin in place. Using the darning needle and the leftover yarn tail, sew the bottom of the Leaf to the Sprout with 3 or 4 whip stitches.

Pin the second Leaf to the Sprout, overlapping the first Leaf by about 4 rnds and matching up the bottom of the Leaves with the htrs pointing upwards. Then attach the second Leaf to the bottom of the Sprout with 3 or 4 whip stitches.

Add the third Leaf to the uncovered side of the Sprout, overlapping the second Leaf by about 4 rnds, then tuck the opposite side of the Leaf under the first Leaf. Before securing, adjust the bottom of the third Leaf to ensure it is tightly pressed with the other two.

Weave the darning needle up through the first overlapping Leaf and add a whip stitch to tack it down so it stays in place. Repeat these steps to secure the other Leaves.

ORNAMENT OPTION

To make a loop to hang the ornament, use a darning needle and either silver or gold crochet thread to add a large loop at the top of the Sprout. Enter the needle on the right side of the magic circle and exit on the left side. Tie the two yarn ends together to complete the loop.

Mince Pie

Adorn your Christmas table with this tasty treat with a rich, festive filling of dried fruits and spices, sure to warm your soul on a cold winter night.

SKILL LEVEL

FINISHED SIZE

2¾ x 1¼in (7 x 3cm)

SUPPLIES AND MATERIALS

Hobbii Rainbow Deluxe 8/4 100% Turkish cotton (approx 186yd/170m per 50g)

1 x 50g ball in 45 Turmeric (A)

1 x 50g ball in 09 Dark Chocolate (B)

Silver or gold crochet thread

2mm (US B/1) crochet hook

Stitch markers

Darning needle

Polyester filling

Scissors

Sewing pins

PATTERN NOTE

Stuff the Pie Crust and Pie Top as you crochet, but do not over-stuff the Pie Top before closing.

PIE CRUST

Rnd 1: With A, working into MC, 6 dc (6 sts).
Rnd 2: (Dc2inc) 6 times (12 sts).
Rnd 3: (1 dc, dc2inc) 6 times (18 sts).
Rnd 4: (1 dc, dc2inc, dc) 6 times (24 sts).
Rnd 5: (3 dc, dc2inc) 6 times (30 sts).
Rnd 6: (2 dc, dc2inc, dc 2) 6 times (36 sts).
Rnd 7: (5 dc, dc2inc) 6 times (42 sts).
Rnd 8: (3 dc, dc2inc, dc 3) 6 times (48 sts).
Rnd 9: BLO 1 dc in each st around (48 sts).
Rnd 10: 1 dc in each st around (48 sts).
Rnd 11: (7 dc, dc2inc) 6 times (54 sts).
Rnds 12 and 13: 1 dc in each st around (54 sts).
Rnd 14: FLO (dc, htr2inc, htr2inc) 18 times (90 sts).
Fasten off and hide the yarn tail inside the Pie Crust.

PIE TOP

Attach B to the first unfinished BLO of rnd 13 of the Pie Crust.
Rnds 15 and 16: 1 dc in each st around (54 sts).
Rnd 17: (7 dc, dc2tog) 6 times (48 sts).
Rnd 18: (3 dc, dc2tog, dc 3) 6 times (42 sts).
Rnd 19: (5 dc, dc2tog) 6 times (36 sts).
Rnd 20: (2 dc, dc2tog, dc 2) 6 times (30 sts).
Rnd 21: (3 dc, dc2tog) 6 times (24 sts).
Rnd 22: (1 dc, dc2tog, dc) 6 times (18 sts).
Rnd 23: (1 dc, dc2tog) 6 times (12 sts).
Rnd 24: (1 dc, dc2tog) 4 times (8 sts).
Weave the yarn under each FLO, pull tight to close the hole.
Fasten off and hide the extra yarn end inside the Pie Top.

STAR

Note: Join the end of each rnd to the first st in the rnd with a sl st.
Rnd 1: With A, working into MC, 10 dc, sl st to the first st to join, 2 ch (13 sts).
Rnd 2: (1 tr, tr2inc) 5 times, sl st, 2 ch (18 sts).
Rnd 3: (1 tr, tr2inc, 1 tr) 5 times, sl st, 2 ch (22 sts).
Rnd 4: (1 dc, htr2inc, 1 tr, 3 ch, dc in third ch from hook, tr in the same st as the first tr, htr2inc) 5 times, sl st to the first dc (56 sts – 5 points).
Fasten off, leaving a long tail for attaching.

ASSEMBLY

Place the Star in the centre of the Pie Top, matching up the five points along rnd 16 of the Pie Top, evenly spaced.

Using the darning needle and the leftover yarn tail from the Star, sew the five points to the Pie Top with a whip stitch on each to secure the Star.

ORNAMENT OPTION

To make a loop to hang the ornament, use the darning needle and either silver or gold crochet thread to add a large loop at the top of the Mince Pie. Enter the needle on the right side of the magic circle and exit on the left side of the magic circle. Tie the two yarn ends together to complete the loop.

Candy Cane

Red-and-white striped candy canes are said to have originated in Germany in the 17th century, when they were given out to children by the choirmaster at Cologne Cathedral to keep them quiet during festive services.

SKILL LEVEL

FINISHED SIZE

4¼in (11cm)

SUPPLIES AND MATERIALS

Hobbii Rainbow Deluxe 8/4 100% Turkish cotton (approx 186yd/170m per 50g)

1 x 50g ball in 001 White (A)

1 x 50g ball in 059 Apple Red (B)

2mm (US B/1) crochet hook

Darning needle

Scissors

Pipe cleaners

PATTERN NOTE

Starting with A, work all stitches in a round. Change colour on the last stitch when instructed. Do not stuff, wire will be added later in the pattern.

CANDY CANE

Rnd 1: With A, working into MC, 4 dc (4 sts).

Rnd 2: (Dc2inc) 4 times (8 sts).

From the next rnd, alternate the colours between A and B.

Rnds 3-9: (2 dc changing to B on the last st, 2 dc changing to A on the last st) twice (8 sts).

Before working rnd 10, take a pipe cleaner, fold it in half, then twist it to make one thick pipe cleaner measuring about 6in (15cm).

Insert the twisted pipe cleaner into the Candy Cane until it reaches the end. Then continue to crochet around the pipe cleaner as follows:

Rnds 10-52: 2 dc, change to B, 2 dc, change to A, 2 dc, change to B, 2 dc, change to A (8 sts).

Cut B and cont rnd 53 with A only.

Rnd 53: (Dc2tog) 4 times (4 sts).

Fasten off and weave A under each of the FLO, then pull tight and hide all the yarn ends inside the Candy Cane. Bend the Candy Cane at about rnd 30 to make the hook to hang on the tree.

Gingerbread House

The most scrumptious of holiday treats is the gingerbread house, a gingerbread dough rolled, cut into shapes, baked and glued into shape with royal icing. The real fun begins when everyone gets together to decorate it with sweet candies.

SKILL LEVEL

●

FINISHED SIZE

5½ x 4in (14 x 10cm)

SUPPLIES AND MATERIALS

For Full Size

Hobbii Rainbow 8/6 100% cotton (approx 115yd/105m per 50g)

1 x 50g ball in 009 Nougat (A)

1 x 50g ball in 001 White (B)

3mm (US C/2 or D/3) crochet hook, cardboard, pencil

For Ornament Size

Hobbii Rainbow Deluxe 8/4 100% Turkish cotton (approx 186yd/170m per 50g)

1 x 50g ball in 06 Mocha Latte (A)

1 x 50g ball in 01 White (B)

Silver or gold crochet thread, 2mm (US B/1) crochet hook

Stitch markers, darning needle, polyester filling, scissors

PATTERN NOTES

The parts of the House are made in rows. Place the first dc in the second st from the hook at the start of a new row. The Wreath is made in rounds.

SIDE WALLS AND FLOOR (MAKE 3)

Row 1: With A, 21 ch, turn (21 sts).
Rows 2-22: 1 dc in each st along, 1 ch, turn (22 sts).
Fasten off and leave a long tail for attaching.
Using the darning needle, weave in the yarn ends.

FRONT AND BACK WALLS (MAKE 2)

Row 1: With A, 21 ch, turn (21 sts).
Rows 2-22: 1 dc in each st along, 1 ch, turn (22 sts).
Row 23: Dc2tog, 16 dc, dc2tog, 1 ch, turn (19 sts).
Row 24: Dc2tog, 14 dc, dc2tog, 1 ch, turn (17 sts).
Row 25: Dc2tog, 12 dc, dc2tog, 1 ch, turn (15 sts).
Row 26: Dc2tog, 10 dc, dc2tog, 1 ch, turn (13 sts).
Row 27: Dc2tog, 8 dc, dc2tog, 1 ch, turn (11 sts).
Row 28: Dc2tog, 6 dc, dc2tog, 1 ch, turn (9 sts).
Row 29: Dc2tog, 4 dc, dc2tog, 1 ch, turn (7 sts).
Row 30: Dc2tog, 2 dc, dc2tog, 1 ch, turn (5 sts).
Row 31: (Dc2tog) twice, 1 ch, turn (3 sts).
Row 32: Dc2tog (1 st).
Fasten off and weave in the yarn ends.

ROOF (MAKE 2)

Row 1: With A, 21 ch, turn (21 sts).
Rows 2 and 3: 1 dc in each st along, 1 ch, turn (21 sts).
Change to B on the last st. Cut A and weave in the yarn end to the Roof.
Row 4: With B, BLO 1 dc in each st along, 1 ch, turn (21 sts).
Row 5: *1 dc, (tr2inc) twice, 1 dc; rep from * 4 times (30 sts).
Cut B and weave in the yarn end to the Roof.
Flip the Roof over so the section in A is facing you.
Attach A to the first st of the leftover FLO of row 3.
Rows 6-9: With A, 1 dc in each st along, 1 ch, turn (21 sts).
Change to B on the last st. Cut A and weave in the yarn end to the Roof.
Row 10: With B, BLO 1 dc in each st along, 1 ch, turn (21 sts).

Row 11: *1 dc, (tr2inc) twice, 1 dc; rep from * 4 times (30 sts).
Cut B and weave in the yarn end to the Roof.
Flip the Roof over so the section in A is facing you.
Attach A to the first st of the leftover FLO of row 9.
Rows 12-15: With A, 1 dc in each st along, 1 ch, turn (21 sts).
Change to B on the last st. Cut A and weave in the yarn end to the Roof.
Row 16: With B, BLO 1 dc in each st along, 1 ch, turn (21 sts)
Row 17: *1 dc, (tr2inc) twice, 1 dc; rep from * 4 times (30 sts).
Cut B and weave in the yarn end to the Roof.
Flip the Roof over so the section in A is facing you.
Attach A to the first st of the leftover FLO of row 15.
Rows 18-21: With A, 1 dc in each st along, 1 ch, turn (21 sts).
Change to B on the last st. Cut A and weave in the yarn end to the Roof.
Row 22: With B, BLO 1 dc in each st along, 1 ch, turn (21 sts).
Row 23: *1 dc, (tr2inc) twice, 1 dc; rep from * 4 times (30 sts).
Cut B and weave in the yarn end to the Roof.
Flip the Roof piece upside down and attach B to the bottom right corner. 19 dc along the two long sides and 14 dc along the short sides, putting dc2inc in each of the four corners. Fasten off and weave in the yarn ends into the Roof piece.

FRONT DOOR

Row 1: With B, 9 ch, turn (9 sts).
Rows 2-15: 1 dc in each st along, 1 ch, turn (9 sts).
Row 16: 1 dc, 1 tr, tr2inc, (dtr2inc) twice, tr2inc, 1 tr, 1 dc (12 sts).
Cont working down the side of the Door and then around the Door, dc approx 36 sts adding dc2inc in each of the two bottom corners.
Fasten off and leave a long tail for attaching.
Using the darning needle, weave in the yarn ends.

WREATH

Rnd 1: With B, 10 ch, sl st to the first ch to join (11 sts).
On the next rnd, the dc sts will be worked around the chain to make a solid ring.
Rnd 2: 22 dc around the ch, sl st to join (23 sts).
Fasten off and leave a long tail for attaching.

WINDOWS (MAKE 2)

Row 1: With B, (11 ch, sl st in the second ch from hook, 9 ch, sl st in the second ch from hook) twice, sl st (45 sts). Fasten off and leave a long tail for attaching.

CARDBOARD INSERTS

Note: Adding cardboard inserts to the inside of the walls is optional but recommended for a larger-sized Gingerbread House. If you're making a smaller, ornament-sized Gingerbread House, the cardboard inserts are not necessary.

Place a crocheted Side Wall and a Front or Back Wall piece on a large piece of cardboard. With a pencil, outline each of the Front Walls twice and the square Side Walls three times. This is so you have two Front/Back wall inserts, two Side Walls and a Floor. With scissors, cut out all five inserts and set aside.

ASSEMBLY

Attach the square Floor piece to the four Wall sides by working 80 dc. Using A, pair up two of the square pieces at the seams and work 20 dc along the BLO and the FLO of the two pieces to connect them. These are the inner loops that are touching each other. Once finished, do not cut yarn.

Next, match up the bottom of the Front Wall to the corner of the next side of the square Floor piece. 20 dc along the BLO of the bottom of the Front Wall and side of the Floor to sew them together. Once finished, do not cut yarn but continue to the next part.

Attach the second square Wall and, last, the Back Wall to complete all four Walls. Make sure the Walls are in the correct sewn position with the two Side Walls opposite each other and the Front and Back Walls opposite each other. Fasten off all the yarn ends and weave them into the Gingerbread House.

To crochet the Side Walls together, attach B to the corner of the Side Wall closest to you and up against the Floor piece. Then, holding that Wall and the next one together, 22 dc up the Walls to connect them. Repeat this step three more times to attach all the Walls together, ensuring that the House is upright. With the darning needle, weave the extra yarn ends through the Walls and hide them inside.

Use pins to secure the Door on the Front Wall, with the bottom of the Door starting at the FLO on the lower part of the Front panel. Pin the top of the Door at row 21 and in the centre of the Front. With the darning needle and the leftover yarn end from the Door, use mattress stitch to attach the Door to the House. Weave in the leftover yarn end into the House once attached.

Pin the Wreath one row above the centre of the Door. Sew on with the darning needle using the Wreath's yarn tail and mattress stitch in four places: top, bottom and both sides only. Weave in the ends.

The Windows will be sewn horizontally to the Side Walls only. Pin the bottom of the Window between rows 5 and 6 and the top between rows 15 and 16, centred on the Wall and leaving about 3 sts between the sides of the Window and the Wall seams. Once in place, whip stitch the third loop of the chains on with the darning needle and the Window yarn ends. Then, using a long cut piece of B, whip stitch a large plus sign or cross in the middle of the Window to finish it off. Knot the two yarn ends in the inside of the House and hide them.

Add small and medium-sized snowflake details on all four sides of the House in random placements. Start by making an X with B and the darning needle, making sure that the entrance and exit of the ends of the X are evenly spaced. Then weave a plus sign on top of the X shape, entering and exiting the needle evenly spaced.

Once finished, tie the ends of the yarn together inside the house to secure them in place. Add as many snowflakes as you want on the four sides of the House.

Starting with the bottom Floor piece, add the five pieces of cardboard to the inside of the Gingerbread House. If any of the cardboard Walls are higher than the crocheted Walls, trim them with scissors. After adding all the cardboard, fill the inside of the House with stuffing.

Pair up the two Roof pieces at the top seams with the scalloped icing detail lying in a downward fashion. Pin the four corners to the four corners of the House. Then with a long cut piece of B and the darning needle,

use mattress stitch to attach the Roof to the top of the Gingerbread House. Before closing the last section of the Roof, add extra stuffing to fill the top sections of the House. Finish mattress-stitching and weave the yarn ends into the Roof.

ORNAMENT OPTION

Omit the cardboard and fill the Gingerbread House with stuffing. Then, with the darning needle and either silver or gold crochet thread, add a large loop at the top of the House to hang from the Christmas tree. Enter the needle on the right side of the centre roof seam and exit on the left side. Tie the two yarn ends together to complete the loop.

The Gallery

First published 2024 by Guild of Master Craftsman
Publications Ltd, Castle Place, 166 High Street, Lewes,
East Sussex BN7 1XU

Text © Jacki Donhou, Josephine Laurin and
Angel Koychev 2024
Copyright in the Work © GMC Publications Ltd, 2024

ISBN 978 1 78494 697 5

A catalogue record for this book is available from
the British Library.

Publisher Jonathan Bailey
Production Manager Jim Bulley
Senior Project Editors Christine Boggis, Jane Roe
Designer Claire Stevens
Illustrator Martin Woodward
Styling Anna Stevens

Colour origination by GMC Reprographics
Printed and bound in China

Picture Credits
Photographs by Andrew Perris, except for on the
following pages: Jacki Donhou: 57, 60, 65, 125, 132;
Josephine Laurin: 39, 109, 113; Angel Koychev: 23;
Snowflakes throughout: Shutterstock.com

TO ORDER A BOOK CONTACT
GMC Publications Ltd, Castle Place,
166 High Street, Lewes, East Sussex,
BN7 1XU, United Kingdom
Tel: +44 (0)1273 488005
www.gmcbooks.com